Creative Therapy for Children in New Families

Angela Hobday, Angela Kirby and Kate Ollier

BPS Blackwell

350 Main Street, Malden, MA 02148-5018, USA
108 Cowley Road, Oxford OX4 1JF, UK
550 Swanston Street, Carlton South, Melbourne, Victoria 3053, Australia
Kurfürstendamm 57, 10707 Berlin, Germany

First published 2002 by The British Psychological Society and Blackwell Publishers
Ltd, a Blackwell Publishing company

Library of Congress Cataloging-in-Publication Data

Hobday, Angela.
    Creative therapy for children in new families / Angela Hobday, Angela
Kirby, and Kate Ollier.
        p.   cm.
Includes bibliographical references and index.
        ISBN 0–631–23600–7
    1. Adopted children—Mental health. 2. Foster children—Mental
health. 3. Child psychotherapy. 4. Play therapy. I. Ollier, Kate.
II. Kirby, Angela. III. Title.
    RJ507.A36 H63 2002
    618.92′8914—dc21
                                                        2002006179

A catalogue record for this title is available from the British Library.

Set in 10 on 12.5 pt Palatino
by Ace Filmsetting Ltd, Frome, Somerset
Printed and bound in Great Britain
by TJ International, Padstow, Cornwall

For further information on
Blackwell Publishing, visit our website:
http://www.blackwellpublishing.com

Contents

Figures

Acknowledgements

Thank you to our families for their patience and support as we have worked on this book. We are very pleased with the illustrations by our junior authors, Josiah, Eliza and Christopher, so thank you also to them. We are also grateful for help with drawings from Nick Thomson, and for some practical testing of instructions by Corinne Dickson and Ken Hobday. Finally, we must not forget to thank Grey Searle, who deserves a special mention for reviewing the final manuscript, which promptly became the penultimate script, following his suggestions of small but important improvements.

Introduction

Working creatively with children who have moved to new families always presents a challenge. The majority of looked after or adopted children have had experiences that have left them wary or defiant towards adults, especially those who wish to help them. They are often well-versed in their rights and well-defended in their approach. Yet these children are the ones who are often the most emotionally needy. They may not have had the opportunity to live within a caring family and experience affection and care prior to their present placement. It would be good if love and good parenting were enough to provide the healing that these children need, but often additional input is needed in the form of a therapeutic approach. Sometimes this can be offered by the carer, but in most cases a therapist will be involved. This book provides information and insights into the problems that these children may experience, as well as therapeutic tools to use with the children.

We have used the term 'carer' to cover foster carers, adoptive parents or carers within a group residential setting. Most of the activities will be appropriate for use where the child is in long-term care, or when the plan is that they should not return to their birth family. However, plans change and it would be possible sometimes to adapt an activity to a new situation. All of the activities are written for both girls and boys, even when an illustration or example appears gender-biased.

This book builds on the information and activities already published in two previous books 'Creative Therapy: Activities with Children and Adolescents' (CT1: Hobday and Ollier, 1998) and 'Creative Therapy 2: Working with

Parents' (CT2: Ollier and Hobday, 1999). Although this book can be used on its own, reference will be made to the two earlier texts.

As with the first book on activities with children and adolescents, the general aim of this book is to encourage creativity in therapy. The activities can be used as part of, or to supplement, many therapeutic approaches and are designed to be tailored to an individual child's needs.

Therapeutic Approach

The authors of this work are mainly used to working within a cognitive or constructive behavioural framework. However, you may recognize a strong systemic flavour to some of the family-type activities, particularly in chapter 3. Our general emphasis on rewarding is particularly relevant with the group of children who have moved between families and often have been in an abusive situation earlier in their lives.

Underlying the need for these activities is the knowledge that children in substitute care generally have undergone trauma, may well have had difficulties in attachment and may be presenting with difficult behaviour problems. Their emotions may be either externalised or held in. They may have many defence mechanisms that have been useful within an abusive situation but are now handicapping them in their lives. Our aim is to provide tools for therapy to help the child overcome these difficulties in a gentle and often fun atmosphere.

How to Use this Book

When studying the contents pages, you will see that we have provided a background chapter (chapter 1). If you are fairly new to this client group or need to brush up on your specialist skills, we would recommend that you treat this as essential background reading. Also, at the beginning of each chapter of activities there is some text to help you put your therapy in context. Reading this will help you to ascertain whether the activity is useful for your stage of therapy with the child or family you are seeing.

It is important to assess the child first before using any of the activities, except perhaps those in, or referenced in, chapter 2 on creating rapport. It is good practice to gain enough information about the child, the child's past and the present family to be able to define your aims in therapy. There is a guide to assessment in our book on working with parents (CT2: Chapter 2). A minimum amount of information needed would be the child's history and family details, past trauma and/or abuse, any problematic behaviour or concerns and any attempted solutions. A fuller description of the sort of difficulties the child may be experiencing follows in chapter 1.

Collating all the above information and gaining rapport with the child and family will help you begin to work out the reasons for the child's difficulties and plan a therapeutic intervention. From there you will be able to judge which activities are most easily adapted for use with the child or family, in accordance with your therapeutic approach and aims for therapy. As with any plan for therapy, you will need to be flexible to meet the needs and changing circumstances of the child.

Many activities will need adaptation to suit the likes and dislikes of the child, so it is useful to collect this information either through one of the activities in chapter 2 or through other rapport-building exercises. You will then have an idea about whether to have, for example, a strong football theme running through therapy or an emphasis on pets.

As in our first book in this series, each activity has been categorized according to the child's needs or the aim of the activity. Some of the activities already have variations that we have found useful. If you use these, be sure to read the instructions under 'Method' in the main activity. Many activities can be useful for more than one difficulty, so you will find suggestions for extra activities from different chapters listed under 'See also'. We have also listed useful activities from our previous titles.

The activities are also given age guidelines. You may find these guidelines rather broad, but children vary a great deal and past experiences may have delayed development in some areas. A brief guide to age and child development, taken from the first Creative Therapy book (CT1), is reproduced in Appendix 3. This guide may help to decide at which level a child may be. Fuller information can be found in Fahlberg (1994, Chapter 2).

During the course of working with the child and family, you will continue to collect more information that will be useful for you in designing a tailor-made therapy. This information can be used to check that you are still using an effective approach. An example would be the child who struggles with activities for his or her age group – when you see how difficult it is for them, you may wish to use simpler activities.

As with all therapy, it is good to review the progress you have made and repeat some of the original assessment activities that you have used with the child. Children who have moved families are likely to need some therapeutic input for a considerable time, so it may be that you review and reassess several times during the course of your intervention.

Length of Activity

You will notice that we have not given an indication of how long each activity will take. This is because children vary greatly in the amount of time they will need. Generally, it will be possible to complete an activity within an hour-long session. Where an activity is likely to stretch over more than one session, we have generally indicated this in the text.

If the child works very slowly, you may need to find a natural break in the activity, indicating what you and the child will do next time to complete it. However, with children who have moved families it is very important to help the children leave behind any difficult feelings that have been aroused, when they complete the session. For example, if you are working with very painful past issues, try to help the child re-orientate to the present before the end of the session. Similarly, if the focus has been on their relationship with adults who are frightening or upsetting to them, try to end the session by talking about familiar, safe people in their lives.

It is a good rule not to attempt more than one new activity in a session, unless two activities are very strongly linked, following on one from another (as indicated in the text). It is also generally useful to review the previous activity from the last session before proceeding to the new one, because this acts as a 'warm up' for the child (helping them to feel less anxious) and re-establishes rapport.

Materials

As with our previous Creative Therapy titles, all the illustrations, worksheets and appendices within this book are copyright free. Some of the materials may need to be enlarged before use. Please note that the rest of the material in this book remains subject to the usual copyright restrictions.

The items required for each activity are clearly stated. If the suggested materials are not available, you may be able to use substitutes. We have repeated here some guidelines for materials, which may be useful for less experienced therapists:

- Children of up to about 11 or 12 years generally enjoy using coloured paper, coloured pencils and colouring pens (e.g. felt-tips, fibre-tips, textas). Make sure you have some colouring pens fine enough for writing as well as for drawing.
- Adolescents may prefer using more adult pens with white paper, or the word processing package on your computer, if you have one.
- Children take pride in their work and like to keep it in their own special

folder that they can take home and bring back to sessions (but do take photocopies for your clinical file).

- Children like to help with photocopying (if possible) so that they know what happens to their work.
- For some activities, you will need safety scissors, thin card and paste (or a gluestick), counters and a dice.
- This book also contains a few activities where you will need juggling balls or three small beanbags.
- Simple glove puppets are useful for role-play and for some of the other activities in this book. Children like it if the puppets have names.
- Playdough or Plasticine is useful for some activities.

The Setting

The activities here do not need a particular setting, and many of them can be used by carers or social workers in the family home. There are many advantages in working therapeutically in a home – e.g. the homely atmosphere is already there, it is usually warm and comfortable and it is possible to gain a greater understanding of the child's own setting. However, there are disadvantages with this client group in that often the topic that comes up is uncomfortable and difficult. It can feel good for a child dealing with such a topic to leave it in the consulting room and return to the safety of home. You may need to judge carefully where it is appropriate to see the child. If there is a place in the home where the child does not usually go, e.g. a carer's study, this may be a suitable place, subject to the carer's consent.

Wherever it is, there may need to be a few props around. Cushions are useful comforters when emotions are running high, as are soft toys. There will need to be somewhere comfortable to sit and draw, where therapist and child can be at the same level. For a younger child doing an activity, it is best to sit by the side of the child to look at a piece of work together. An older child who talks more may appreciate being sat almost opposite but at a slight angle (4 o'clock position) so that eye contact is not threatening or obligatory.

When you are working with a whole family, make sure you have enough chairs even for the younger children who may become bored of sitting on the floor or on the carer's lap. Because they will find it difficult to concentrate for the whole session, you will need a few toys or colouring materials for them, but it is important to include them when you can if you are using a family approach.

Supervision

Working with children who are talking through or disclosing losses, separation, rejection or other past difficulties may trigger memories in the therapist. The impact of the children's stories and emotions can often cause distress to the therapist.

It is therefore extremely important that you have access to, and use, appropriate personal supervision and support. In addition, even very experienced therapists need supervision to gain the extra viewpoint on the needs of the child and the best approach to be taken.

Format of Sessions

Working with children who have moved to a different family is likely to involve some individual work with the child. However, the early assessment appointments may also include the carers. At some time during the course of therapy, the needs of the whole receiving family will have to be addressed for the work with the child to have the most impact. Therefore, if you are a therapist, it is always useful to have some sessions with the foster carers or adoptive parents on their own. If you are the carer using this book, you may find it useful to use a facilitator, perhaps a family friend or social worker, to help you work through some of the family tasks in this book. Family sessions with the whole receiving family can be useful in creating a new balanced family unit.

When activities are used in the session with the child on their own, it is good practice to ask the child's permission to feed back to the carer. This feedback is best done with the child present. This is when you and the child together can explain why you have done the task and encourage the child to tell the carer about it, if they are happy to do so. Not only will it give you the opportunity to see what the child has understood from the session, but it will also prepare the carer for any difficulties that arise because of the nature of the information that the child has worked on in the session. Additionally, it will give you the opportunity to discuss with the carers how to help the child if feelings are externalized at home because of the content of the session. The child may or may not want the carer to know what has happened in the session but try to prepare the carer in any case. This may be by explaining that you have covered difficult subjects in the session so the child may need more support during the coming weeks, working through the emotions.

The task may lend itself to homework. If so, it is good to explain this to the carers as well as the child. It is important to make it clear that any homework is not obligatory, but is useful and will help you to help the child. Try not to give homework that will give rise to raw emotions; this work is best done in the safe setting of the sessions.

If you are a carer using these activities with the child, try to create a 'session'. Choose a time of day that does not interfere with favourite television programmes or activities, and a place that is either away from your home or is in a part of the home that is 'separate' for the child, as mentioned earlier. This will help the work to feel finished, and left in that room at the end of the session, so that the child can resume everyday activities without interference from emotions that have arisen in the session.

Level of Prompting

As for the activities in our previous book on working with children (CT1), the level of prompting for the activities will depend on the ability and personality of the child. Many of the instructions for the activities contain indicators as to how or when to encourage the child to give further information. As a general guide, younger children will cope better with choosing between a few offered suggestions, whereas those around 8 or 9 years old will be able to manage prompts that ask for examples. Teenagers will usually be able to respond to more open-ended questions if they are socially skilled and have established a good rapport. Initially, though, even older teenagers may benefit from a younger approach as they begin to gain confidence in using the sessions. It is worth noting when a usually forthcoming child is finding a task difficult. This may mean that the subject matter is too painful, that they have not understood what is required or something has made them angry.

General Tips for Working with Children

In order for this book to stand alone, we are repeating the general tips that readers have found useful from the previous books. Some others are added that are particularly relevant to this client group. Remember that every child needs an individual approach and that these children may be particularly sensitive to difficult issues. For children who have undergone separation and losses, trusting adults may be difficult. It may take longer to establish trust with them when in a therapeutic relationship. In some cases, you may find that the child works better with you when the carer is in the room. That having been said, the following may apply:

- Some children will want to do the writing themselves and others will want you to be their 'secretary'. It is best to offer them a choice.
- Remember that the resources are only useful when the child is having fun and is taking an active role. If the child is not interested, it is better to use an alternative activity.
- Let the child have as much control over the tasks as possible, e.g. choosing colours and deciding on the layout and style, if you are doing the writing.
- If children are anxious about working in front of you, it will help them to participate if you do it imperfectly first. For example, once you have drawn very basic stick men, you will generally find that they want to draw something a bit more exciting.
- Children have a right to confidentiality within legal bounds – discuss with them before talking to their carers or social workers about their work. Explain to the children what will happen to their file of work, especially if there are legal issues about contact or placement.
- Be prepared to cope if the child becomes upset through dealing with very sensitive issues. A box of tissues needs to be handy and you may need to be ready to bring in the carer to comfort the child.
- Some children may find a therapeutic environment and their therapist threatening. This may be demonstrated by the child's behaviour being physically destructive and aggressive. In this instance it could be helpful to establish some ground rules with them. For example, you could say that it is important that you know how they are feeling but some behaviours, like hitting or kicking, are not acceptable. You could even draw up a list of 'Rules for this Room', including on it the rewards that will be given for acceptable behaviour.
- Making therapy fun will help to relax children so that they are more likely to open up to you.
- A few children's jokes up your sleeve may help (but make sure they are good, clean, fun and will not sound like something else by the time the children tell the joke to their carers in their own unique way!).
- For filling in charts at home, involve the children in ticking boxes, applying stickers or even designing and colouring forms, if they would like to do this. This will help them feel in control of the programme. Always make sure they know exactly what they need to do to earn a tick or sticker.
- Always try to have your materials ready before the session, or at least within easy reach.
- Try to make a link between sessions by referring to a hopefully non-emotive item that the child raised in the previous session, e.g. 'I see you are wearing your favourite colour today'.

Areas Covered by the Book

The subject of children who have moved to new families is vast and complicated. We have outlined many of the difficulties that children have and the reasons for these difficulties. The activities we have introduced here, and some from our previous books, can be part of a programme designed to help the child overcome these difficulties. We have tried to introduce activities that will suit the majority of children who have moved families and hope that activities can be adjusted to an individual child's circumstances. Although many of the activities focus on the child, it is important to engage with and involve the carers. Indeed, other professionals, such as social workers, play a large part in the decisions and care of the looked after child. Therefore, it is often important to consider taking an even wider systems approach to include all relevant professionals working with the child and family.

It is outside the scope of this book to include activities regarding reintegration to the birth family or other issues surrounding the birth parents' own feelings, etc. Also, we have focused more on the child than the receiving family while recognizing that carers and the carers' family may have their own losses and adjustment difficulties. These topics are covered more fully by the authors of the recommended texts in the Further Reading list.

A Word of Warning

This is a book of useful therapeutic activities, but the activities themselves do not constitute a therapeutic programme. Although some of the activities could be used by a foster carer or adoptive parent, this is unlikely to be enough on its own. Children who have moved between families very often need some independent therapy, and the dual role of carer and therapist is very difficult to maintain. Therefore, difficult emotional issues and challenging behaviours are more likely to respond to therapeutic help from a trained clinical psychologist or other specialist therapist. The activities in this book are best used as tools to meet specific goals within specific therapies.

Chapter 1

Setting the Scene

Looked after or adopted children have the same needs for parenting as any other child. However, their past experiences may have led to them being unable to benefit from even the best parenting. This leads to the foster carers or adoptive parents feeling frustrated and de-skilled. In this chapter we will outline some of the problems that commonly arise for children who have moved families, putting these in the context of the underlying psychological factors. This should give us a better understanding of the nature of the child's difficulties and help find the appropriate therapeutic intervention to suit the child.

Problems with Attachment

Attachment is described as 'an affectionate bond between two individuals that endures through space and time and joins them emotionally' (Klaus and Kennell, 1976). Attachment is usually formed in a very young child with a first caregiver and is very important, providing the foundation for a child's overall emotional, physical, intellectual and social development. Bowlby (1995) has described how a child's early attachment experiences can shape the behaviour, interactions and expectations in future relationships. He suggests that children form internal working models of how their attachment figures communicate and behave towards them and in turn how they interact with them. Models become established as cognitive representations that influence all future relationships (Main et al., 1985). It is recommended that the reader refer to Bowlby for further information about this complex area.

Even if children were able to form an attachment with their original primary caregiver, they may have experienced breaking attachments with significant others when they moved into care or changed placements. If a child has not had the opportunity to form a good attachment, emotional and psychological disturbances are likely to occur, e.g. anxiety, depression and anger. In some cases, the child could be described as having reactive attachment disorder (American Psychiatric Association, 1994), a diagnosis based on the child's past history and the clinician's observation of such factors as lack of eye contact, withdrawal, control battles, chronic anxiety, aggressive behaviour or delayed development of a conscience.

Howe and his colleagues (1999) describe how individual children present in different ways when there has been no or poor attachment. They describe how some children present as 'ambivalent/coercive', others as 'avoidant/ defended' and yet others as 'disorganized/controlling'. These differences in presentation give us important clues for an understanding of the child's therapeutic needs.

There are activities in this book that have been designed to help build positive attachments. However, although it is important that attachment difficulties should be addressed, because they are so fundamental to child development, it is often not possible to reach the children until some of the other areas of difficulty in their lives have been at least partially resolved.

Problems from Abusive Experiences

Children who have been placed in care may well have been placed because of some form of abuse within the birth family. They may have symptoms of post-traumatic stress, e.g. nightmares, flashbacks and intrusive thoughts. Also, to survive within abusive situations children will have developed tactics that are functional in protecting them. Once out of the abusive situation the survival tactics are no longer needed, but by then they have been integrated into the child's ways of interacting with the world. Examples of survival tactics and difficulties are outlined in table 1.1.

When looking at the list of survival tactics, it is hardly surprising that the long-term effects of child abuse as summarized by Stevenson (1999) include: attachment difficulties, lower IQ, external locus of control, delays in language acquisition, problems in social relationships and increased risk of suicide, alcohol abuse and anxiety. Although being placed in a stable caring environment will provide the right background for change, children who have been abused often need therapeutic help as well.

Therapists can help children to understand their feelings and promote the development of trust that can lead to building attachments and appropriate

Table 1.1 Problems experienced by abused children

Survival tactics	Problems
Disassociation from body signals	Abnormal response to pain, eating problems, toilet problems
Normalizing the abuse	Inappropriate sexual behaviour, relationship problems, bullying
Manipulation/control	Bossy/over-assertive, friendship problems
Self-blame	'Too-good' behaviour, difficulties protecting self, self-abuse, low self-esteem
Retreat into fantasy world	Ignoring others, concentration problems
Watchfulness	Distrust, fears

friendships. Also, children may need to learn and understand appropriate sexual boundaries and how to keep safe. A focused intervention may be needed for specific behaviours, e.g. to begin to overcome poor eating habits or to regain lost toileting skills. But probably the most important task of therapists will be to help the child survivors of abuse to build a positive sense of identity and rediscover how to value themselves.

Separation, Loss and Rejection

Children who have moved families have left behind people with whom they may have formed good or negative attachments. They also leave behind friends, toys, pets, extended family, school, homes and sometimes status. As a result of this they may be cautious about new relationships, and experience normal grief reactions to their losses. Sadness felt by children because of their losses can be expressed as anger and disobedience. In addition, their fear of loss may lead them to test new relationships or distrust others to the extent that they develop separation anxiety with their new carers. The testing of boundaries can be seen as an attempt to establish the new carer's stability and seek to ensure that however badly the child behaves they will not be rejected again. Building a more positive attachment and introducing claiming behaviours will help the child to be less fearful.

Comparison between carers, or fantasized previous carers and the present carers, may take place. This can lead to a 'birth family shadow', a term coined by Hajal and Rosenberg (1991). The phrase refers to the way a child carries memories and an image of the birth family that affects relationships, bonds and expectations within the new family. This may be very obvious when a child says something like 'My old mum always let me run across the road', but can be far less overt. Similarly, the new carers will be aware of former bonds and feelings. This can cause difficulties in the forming of relationships with a child. The therapist will need to assist the child and carers to separate out the past and to build new relationships and expectations based on the present.

However, some behavioural difficulties experienced by children who have suffered loss and rejection are at a much deeper level than testing boundaries or comparing carers. The child may be caught up in past experiences and emotions that appear to be out of his or her conscious control. They may experience affect flashbacks where the flashback is not about an aversive experience but the original incident has gathered emotional meaning over time. These incidents can be described as 'timeholes' (Hobday, 2001). The therapist will need to help the child and family recognize what is going on psychologically, and build the child's confidence by acknowledging feelings and providing reassurance, until the timeholes diminish.

For the child who is suffering loss, past relationships need to be acknowledged, but this in itself can cause difficulties for children who may have problems resolving the ambivalence they feel (Brinich, 1990). Such ambivalence is experienced when the child is struggling with hating and loving at the same time. For example, an adoptive son may feel that he can only love his adoptive parents if he hates his birth parents, and vice versa. This can result in behavioural difficulties whenever contact visits, or even good memories of his birth family, disrupt the forming of his new attachments.

The role of the therapist may be to work through the loss issues in order to bring the child to some resolution. Additionally, there will be the need to help the child acknowledge the feelings that are being experienced and understand that it is possible to feel positively about birth parents (or former foster carers) at the same time as feeling positive about the present carers. The child will also need to learn that it is all right to feel angry about what has happened and to recognize that both angry and loving feelings are possible towards important people in his or her life.

Recreating Old Patterns

Children's lives are peppered with routines and patterns. Many of these are good tools for reducing anxiety, e.g. tucking a child up in bed and giving him or her a kiss before leaving them. However, many children who have lived in a care-impoverished environment have become used to aversive routines that reduce their anxiety. For example, such children may have learnt that if they screamed loud enough they would gain their parent's attention, and, even though this was accompanied by a smack, it felt familiar. Unfortunately, the need for a child to recreate similar aversive experiences within the new family can present enormous challenges to the new carers. The therapist's focus needs to be upon helping the family recognize and resist the aversive patterns and establish new routines and ways of gaining attention and reducing anxiety.

Other patterns of behaviour may be linked to past abuse or poor parenting. For example, a child may have had to parent a younger sibling. This can lead to bossy, over-assertive behaviour and perhaps an undermining of the new carers when they try to parent the younger child. Here the therapist may focus the work with the parenting child on beginning to gain a wider understanding of families and enjoying the younger sibling as a sister or brother.

Developmental Problems

As mentioned above, poor attachment can lead to developmental problems. Additionally, the child's cognitive development will be 'on hold' each time the child moves families, when the most important psychological task is adjusting to the new placement and overcoming loss. There may be time lost in school and there is often a change of school. It is not surprising that the Department of Health (1991) reported poor educational achievement as one of the factors that impairs the life chances of looked after children. Although the therapist, social worker or carer may not be able to address the child's educational needs, it is important to be aware of the difficulties and perhaps have close liaison with school, contributing to multi-disciplinary meetings as appropriate.

Social development may be affected by the break in relationships and attachment difficulties. Past abuse may be a cause of poor social skills, as outlined above. Here therapy may have a role, not only in helping to build positive attachments but also in developing social skills.

Summary

We have outlined above some of the difficulties that children who have moved families may present. However, when working with these children it can sometimes be a challenge to disentangle their difficulties. The effects of their past can be seen clearly, but the causes cannot be so neatly understood. To focus completely on the cause may not be as important as addressing the children's present-day needs, helping them to find their own identity and form good attachments. Then, as you work with the child, it will probably become easier to identify the underlying causes of the behaviour. Even with children who are not in a secure long-term placement, it is possible to help them become more sure of themselves and build resilience and skills to help them cope in future situations.

Chapter 2

Getting to Know You

Children who have moved between families often have to be encouraged to participate in therapy. They have seen too many adults in their lives, some of whom have appeared to betray their confidences by moving them away from the family. The activities in this chapter are primarily designed to assist you to help them overcome any reticence and to build a good rapport with the child. However, you will see that some of the activities can be adapted for use at other stages in your therapy.

Meet the Star (Age: 4–13 years)

AIM

To help establish rapport and to provide an opportunity for the child to get used to talking about him or herself in a therapeutic setting. To pro-vide in-formation about the child's likes and dislikes and to begin to access his or her thoughts. It will also give some insight as to how the child sees him or herself. This activity can be used before 'Today's Star Guest' (see next activity).

MATERIALS

A3 or A4 paper, colouring pens and pencils, glitter pen (optional).

Method

Explain to the child that you want to learn more about him or her and that one way to do this would be to make a poster about him or herself. Explain that you could pretend that the child is going to be a star guest on the radio or TV and that the poster will 'advertise' him or her. You want it to capture the public's attention!

Write 'Meet the Star' at the top of the page. Younger children could draw a picture of themselves in the centre of the page whereas older children could write their name (if you have a glitter pen, all the better!).

Around the picture or name explain that you are going to write some important things about them to give the public some headlines. Give them a few ideas by asking them some non-threatening questions such as 'What is your favourite game? What are you good at?' Use their responses to frame your questions. To keep this positive you may need to help a child who struggles to identify positive attributes. Help the children choose which things they want to put on their posters. They may want to write or draw them or they may ask you to write, so be guided by the children but let them do as much of it as they comfortably can.

If this activity is to be used before 'Today's Star Guest' you could write 'Tune in next week to find out more' at the bottom of the page.

Our example (figure 2.1) shows the work of a 7-year-old.

Variation: Our Star Feature (Age: 12 years and upwards)

An adolescent may be more interested in writing a short piece about him or herself, as if for a popular magazine or a magazine listing radio programmes if the following activity is also to be used. Encourage the adolescent to describe his or her interests, personality, skills, etc. Be prepared to do much of the writing down yourself, if necessary. This piece of work could be written up on a computer, with appropriate graphics or heading styles.

Help the child to make this piece of writing sparky, exciting and up-to-date. End it either with 'Tune in next week. . .', as in the main activity, or a reference to more exciting information about the adolescent to come in later issues of the magazine.

See also

- Feelings Spinning Wheel (p. 55)
- Strings of Feelings (p. 57)

Figure 2.1   Meet the Star

- Feelings Basket (p. 58)
- Just Me (p. 44)
- My World (CT1, p. 11)

Today's Star Guest (Age: 8–14 years)

Aim

To put the child at ease and begin to build rapport. This activity also aims to help you gain information from the child about likes, dislikes, thoughts and feelings. It can be used later on in therapy to talk about past experiences, or future hopes and dreams.

Materials

A tape recorder with a hand-held microphone and tape cassette (or a toy microphone, or something that can imitate one). Pen and paper.

Method

Before you begin the session you will need to work out the questions you would like to ask the child. This will depend on whether you are using the exercise to begin to get to know the child or whether you are using it at another stage in therapy.

Explain to the child that you are going to pretend to be on the radio or television and that you will be the interviewer and interview him or her. Make sure that the child understands that you will not be submitting the tape to be broadcast! You may need to decide with the child whether he or she would like you to be interviewed first. This is a tricky one, as you will not want to disclose your personal life, but you may be able to provide the child with a few questions to ask you 'for practice'.

Arrange all your equipment and test it. Make a play of recording 'testing, testing' and making it fun. Do not worry if it takes some time to set up – use the time to laugh and joke with the child to help reduce anxiety. You are now ready to begin the 'interview'. Set it up by making an over-the-top announcement, with a flourish. For example, 'Welcome to today's star guest, Simon Smith. We are extremely privileged to have Mr Smith with us today, taking him away from his very busy and important schedule. We look forward to hearing him tell us many interesting things about his life and the way he sees the world. Let's all give a big hand to our star guest.' Clap loudly at this point, smiling and encouraging the child.

Start asking your questions in a light, interviewing manner. The first questions need to be very easy to answer and very non-threatening. For example, 'Please could you tell our listeners how old you are?' Lead on to the more crucial questions later, if the child relaxes into the game and seems to be enjoying him or herself. Supplement the questions with statements like 'Our listeners may like to know that Mr Smith is wearing a sweatshirt advertising a good football club. Would you like to tell the listeners which club you support and why?'

If this is the first time you have used this activity with the child, it may be good to keep it short, asking less than ten questions. If the child enjoys using this format, you can extend the interviews on subsequent occasions. In any case, be careful not to make the interview so long that the child becomes bored. End the interview with suitable phrases. For example, 'Thank you Mr Smith for your valuable and interesting contribution to our programme. We look forward to hearing more from you in the future.' The child will probably want to hear the tape once you have finished. Use this opportunity to talk through anything the child has said, and check its accuracy if you need to. Always do this in a non-threatening manner so that the child does not feel that he or she is being doubted.

For your own records, do not forget to listen to the tape after the session and make notes. Keep the tape ready for the next session when the child will probably want to hear it again.

S<small>EE ALSO</small>

- Just Me (p. 44)
- My Story (p. 101)
- Snappy Choices (p. 50)

Connecting Questions (Age: 6–12 years)

A<small>IM</small>

To encourage rapport and help the child to give snippets of information about him or herself.

M<small>ATERIALS</small>

'Connect 4' (MB Games, Hasbro International) or similar simple shop-bought game that is quick to play and where the therapist and child can take turns. Pen and paper.

METHOD

Use the rules of the game to have a practice run through. Just play the game through first time round. Next explain that this time we are going to make it into a more useful game, and you will ask the child a question before you have your go, and the child will give you the answer before having his or her go.

Start with easy questions, like where the child lives or the names of siblings. Go through once with questions about general life, and then next time round you will be able to focus on talking about feelings. If this is early on in therapy, you will be able to just take it in turns thinking of feelings.

Variation: Feelings Focus

Later on in therapy, you may wish to use the game to discuss specific feelings (e.g. 'being angry') when the child has to tell you about times when the feelings have been experienced. If you are using the game in this way, it is important to end with a positive feeling. If the child cannot answer the last question, find another positive feeling. For example, if you have said 'happy' and no response is forthcoming, try asking when the child has felt 'pleased'. If that is still too difficult, find a neutral feeling, e.g. 'sleepy', and then try to extract from the child's answer some positive thoughts or feelings.

SEE ALSO

- Feelings Spinning Wheel (p. 55)
- Strings of Feelings (p. 57)
- Feelings Basket (p. 58)
- Snappy Choices (p. 50)
- My World (CT1, p.11)
- Happy, Sad, Angry (CT1, p.17)
- Feelwheel (CT1, p.25)

Telling Trivia (Age: 9–14 years)

AIM

To create a fun-like atmosphere where the child contributes information.

Materials

Approximately 20 prepared cards with suitably worded questions. Pen and answer sheet (see figure 2.2) for each player. Playing board (see figure 2.3).

Method

Designed for two players (child and therapist), this game requires a great deal of preparation but can be used over again for other children.

Prepare questions clearly written on small cards (approximately playing card size). Have three answer sheets ready for each player. Prepare a playing board, preferably on card and laminated if you wish to use it again.

For some children, and in some settings, it may be possible to make the playing board together. However, the questions may need to be kept secret from the child until the game is played, to avoid discussion of the answers beforehand, which would sabotage the game.

The questions should be worded along the following lines: 'What is the other player's favourite colour?' The aim of the game is to make accurate guesses, or use your previous knowledge of the child to get the answers right. Depending upon the ability of the child, you can introduce some more complicated therapeutic questions, e.g. 'If the other player were a tree, what sort of tree would he like to be'. To keep the game moving forward, have some questions with a very narrow choice to increase the chances of the answers being correct. For example, 'Does the other player prefer cats or dogs as pets?' A number up to six should be on the corner of each card, roughly relating to the difficulty of the question – the higher the number, the more difficult the question. If the game is being played by the therapist with the child, the question subjects may need to be chosen carefully to keep appropriate boundaries.

The question is read out and both players write down the topic of the question in the column marked 'Category'. One word will do, to identify the question later (e.g. 'colour','tree'or 'pets', for the questions indicated above). The other player writes down the answer in the column headed 'True' on their answer sheet, while the person whose question it is writes their guess under 'Guess'. Then compare your results. If the guess is correct, move forward the number of spaces indicated on the card. If it is wrong, move back that number. If either of you land on a square with an instruction, obey that instruction. Put the cards to the bottom of the pile as you use them – once you have been through them once, put the answer sheets out of sight and start fresh ones. This time round the answers will be easier (if no-one changes their responses) and therefore quicker.

Telling Trivia Answer Sheet

Category	True	Guess

Figure 2.2   Telling Trivia Answer Sheet

Your answer sheet can act as a record of the child's answers, if you are always careful to write down the 'true' replies. The information you gain can be used in your future sessions with the child to prepare suitable materials that you know appeal to the child.

The winner is the person who reaches 'finish' first. With children with low self-esteem, it may be diplomatic to give them a chance to win until you know them well enough to work on the problems they have with losing.

Variation: Tell the Group Trivia

This game can be used in a group setting, with several children. You will not need to play, but can act as facilitator. If you wish to use the answer sheet to record each child's responses, then it may be helpful to use different colours for each child and provide yourself with a key.

For a group, each prepared card should have questions on it that can be asked about the next person to play. All can guess, and all move according to

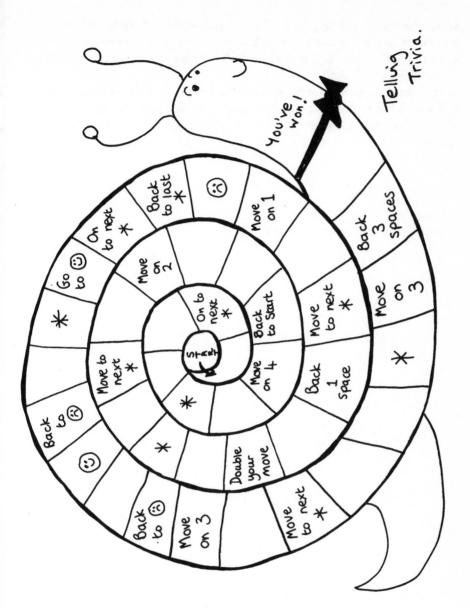

Figure 2.3   Telling Trivia Gameboard

the correctness of their guess. The playing board will need to have more squares than the one illustrated or the game may be over before all the players have had a turn. You will also need more cards – up to eight cards per player will be sufficient.

In a group, you may find that you have to help and encourage any shy or reticent children. They may be more ready to participate if you allow them to write down their answers, ready for you to read them out to the rest of the group.

SEE ALSO

● Snappy Choices (p. 50)
● Personal Pursuits (CT1, p. 76)

Chapter 3

Creating a New Family

Children going into a new family have to learn fast. There are family routines and rules that are individual to each family and sometimes can be quite rigid. The accommodating family may find it difficult to adapt to the needs of the child and to make explicit the implicit rules that have made the family what it is. Fitting the child into the existing family system is not likely to work; there will need to be changes in roles and in the way the family works. It is not only the carers who will have to adjust. Any other children in the family also will be affected. As the title suggests, the activities in this chapter are designed to speed up the process of integrating the child into the family and helping the family to understand the need to change, in order to accept and include the child.

Order! (Age: 6 years and upwards)

Aim

To help the family notice characteristics about each other, including the incoming child. To have fun together. To gain information about the family members and the family system.

Materials

Pen and paper to make notes. Enough space for the family to move about. Prepared cards.

METHOD

This is a family game that should only need a little organizing and it will then take off. If all the children are over 10 years old, you may be able to fade into the background to assume the role of observer.

Explain to the family that part of getting to know everyone is to see how they relate to everyone else. This is not just how they get on with each other, but includes other areas such as looks and height.

Ask everyone to stand up, and then someone picks a category card with a category on it. The person who has picked the card then has to arrange the rest of the family in that order, without telling them what is on the card. The family members then have to guess what is on the card. For younger children you will probably need to help.

Example categories could include:

- Loudest to quietest
- Largest to smallest shoe size
- Most funny to most serious
- Most argumentative to most easygoing
- Tallest to smallest
- Biggest smile to smallest smile
- Most hair to least hair
- Curliest hair to straightest hair

Avoid using categories that may be sensitive, such as nastiest to nicest, or meanest to most generous. Also avoid areas such as fattest to thinnest or cleverest to dimmest. It is best to prepare categories beforehand because otherwise children may well think up categories that may be detrimental to your therapy!

Feed back to the family some positive responses to the way they have worked. Include everyone, even if you have to resort to saying that some of the family were 'really enjoying themselves' or were 'especially good at noticing when the game was going on for too long'.

Variation: Redro! (Age: 10 years and upwards)

'Redro' is order back to front, so this game is best played once Order! is well established. It is best done with families who are quite positive towards each other, to be sure that negative aspects of a particular family member are not focused upon. Once the family is familiar with Order!, it can be played the other way round. One member of the family puts the family in random order and then the family try to think up a way in which they are ordered. This is quite hard, and they may need to resort to factors such as 'In order of who is nearest the door'. Keep changing the order until there have been several different combinations, some of which will yield easy to work out answers such as 'noisiest to quietest'.

SEE ALSO

- Family Questions (CT1, p.113)
- Who's Who (CT1, p.106)

Family Web (Age: 6 years and upwards)

AIM

To help the family find some interests or other features of family members that are similar to those of the incoming child.

MATERIALS

Prepared cards with topics. Large sheet of paper (A2 or A3), colouring pens and ruler.

METHOD

This activity is best done on the second or a subsequent session with you. You will then be able to use some of your knowledge of the family and looked after or adoptive child to prepare cards with topics that can be used to illustrate sameness.

Explain to the family that everyone is different and likes different things. However, there are some things that everyone likes and others that only one or two people like. Similarly, there are some things about people's looks or skills that are the same and some that are different.

On the large piece of paper, write everyone's name near the edge, well spaced out (see figure 3.1). You will need a bit of a space in the middle. Shuffle the prepared topic cards. Let one of the children take a card and read it out, or help them read it. Then under each person's name write briefly about the subject. For example, if the topic is 'hair colour', then 'blonde hair' or 'black hair', etc. may be written under each person's name. When you have finished using the cards, ask the family to think of other subjects or choose some yourself. Try to focus on any topics where the incoming child has similar characteristics.

When you have several topics under each name, discuss the collection of characteristics and likes/dislikes with the family. Let them take turns in noticing any things that are in common with two or more people and, using colouring pens, link up those items. It may help to use a ruler for this part of the activity.

Your final piece of work should look very colourful and should have illustrated several areas where the incoming child is similar to other people in the family. If anyone starts to count who has the most, try to discourage that, saying that there must be many more things but we can't think of everything today. The activity could lead on to a discussion about ways in which members of the family can work and share together, e.g. by encouraging the incoming child to take up a hobby that is already enjoyed by someone else in the family. Alternatively the whole family could agree to become involved in something that the incoming child enjoys, thus giving the message that the child's preferences are appreciated.

Example items are:

- Hair colour
- Hobbies
- Favourite colour
- Favourite toy
- One thing I hate
- Best day of the week
- Favourite clothes
- Football team most want to support
- Sort of holiday liked best
- Favourite television programme
- Shoe size
- Month of birthday
- Length of hair
- Favourite type of film

SEE ALSO

- Who's Who (CT1, p.106)

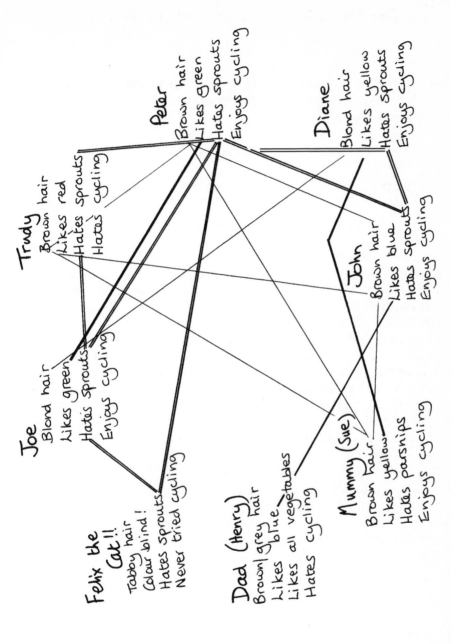

Figure 3.1 Family Web

Our Family Rules (Age: 5 years and upwards)

Aim

To make explicit the implicit family rules to help the incoming child understand how the family works. To promote discussion about how rules help a family to live together.

Materials

Thin card, pen, scissors, up to four sheets of A4 paper.

Method

Before the session, prepare a list of very silly, implausible family rules along with some serious ones. If possible, try to make even some of the serious ones sound a little bit like fun. If there are some rules that have come up in previous sessions, or from your prior knowledge of the family, be sure to include these. Do not include any punitive rules.

Write all the rules onto thin card and cut them out, so that one rule is on each piece of card. The number of rules you have will depend on how long you want the activity to take and the amount of time you think you will be able to keep everyone's interest in the game. The wording on the cards will need to take account of the age and understanding of the children in the family. If you want to focus on a particular area of family functioning, you may wish to keep the number of serious cards quite low, but keep several implausible, or at least less serious, ones to keep the game light-hearted.

Be sure to include everyone in the discussion in this activity. Sometimes the incoming child is very aware of implicit family rules, having had good practice at watching out for them in previous placements. However, at other times this activity could make the child feel excluded, so be sure to be sensitive to this and direct the activity accordingly.

Rules to select may include:

Serious rules

- All toys or tools to be put away after use
- Everyone knows where the others are
- Everyone says when they will be home in the evenings
- Everyone respects each other

- No arguing at the dinner table
- Pets must be kept downstairs (or, no-one with four legs allowed upstairs)
- No muddy shoes in the best room
- Only invisible handprints can go on the wall
- No leaving the table before we have all finished
- All children in bed by 9 p.m. (or, peace for all parents by 9 p.m.)
- Everyone helps clear the table after a meal

Silly rules

- Everyone must slide down the banisters twice a day
- No laughing indoors
- No-one can eat custard unless they've eaten jelly first
- Gloves and hats must be worn at breakfast
- Everyone walks backwards on Tuesdays

Introduce the activity to the family by explaining about how sometimes rules are very clear, e.g. the rules about driving a car or wearing school uniform. At other times there are rules that you do not know you have broken until you are in trouble or have upset someone. Explain that every family has rules but they are not usually written down. Today's activity aims to help everyone understand some of the rules this family has, and to talk about any that they are not sure about.

The family members take turns to pick a rule. The family then discuss it and write it under 'Our Family Rules' or 'Not Our Rules' on separate sheets of paper. Be prepared to start a third category on another sheet, named 'Under Discussion' or 'Preferred But Not Rules'. Try to use this section only as a last resort, or else everything will go in it!

When you have run out of rules, try to encourage the family to come up with some of their own. If they come up with punitive rules (e.g. 'children shall be smacked if they come downstairs after they have been sent to bed'), then try to reword it to bring out the essence of the aimed-for behaviour. For example, 'All children to stay upstairs after their bedtime'. Be sure to make a note elsewhere of the punitive nature of the contribution, to work on this with the carer or child at an appropriate time.

Suggest to the family that the 'Our Family Rules' list goes home with them, and is displayed prominently. This activity is mainly to inform, but the family may want to discuss what to do if people do not keep the rules. In that case, encourage them to turn that around to rewarding them for keeping rules they find difficult.

Variation: Sticking to Rules (Age: 8 years and upwards)

This version is based on the activity 'Our Family Rules', but it is mad more of a family game. Instead of writing the rules on thin card, they ne be written on sticky labels. Start with a few rules ready prepared. Then at a time, a rule is stuck onto a family member's back, without him c seeing it. The others then give clues as to what the rule is, and the rule-t has to guess the rule. Once the rule is guessed, it is discussed and the ru be simply stuck onto the lists (or written on if it will not re-stick!). Rem to include some silly rules in this version.

When you have run out of rules, encourage the family members to their own rules on a sticky label and stick it on someone else's back. The at a time, they have to ask other people questions until they can work out the rule says. Alternatively, have everyone do it together. As the therapis you can facilitate by ensuring that no-one is unsure what to do, or is getting stressed because they cannot guess. You can even add a few clues of your own to help anyone who is stuck. As family members guess their own, encourage them to help others who have not yet guessed. Once all are guessed, work through them and write them on the appropriate pieces of paper as before.

SEE ALSO

- Family Rules (CT1, p.108)

We are a Team (Age: 8 years and upwards)

AIM

To encourage all the family members to appreciate how they can work to-gether, and give the incoming child an understanding of how he or she is already a member of the family team.

MATERIALS

Prepared list of co-operative family tasks, large sheet of paper, colouring pens.

METHOD

Explain to the family that today's theme is teamwork. Encourage them to talk about any teams they are involved in, outside the family, e.g. the school football team, a darts team or the team who make the refreshments at Church. Lead this on to talk about everyone in the household (family) working together in various ways because they are part of a team. Sometimes everyone works together on a particular task (e.g. everyone clearing up after a meal). Alternatively, sometimes everyone may be doing different things to work towards a particular goal. For example, the family may want a quiet afternoon at home, so John agrees to keep the television volume down low, Sally and Sue agree not to quarrel, Dad says he'll play cards with the girls and Mum says she'll light the fire for them all to sit by.

This leads you on to introduce the game. One family member, e.g. Sally, is given a task off the list and then has to set each member of the family to mime it, without telling them what the task is. To do this, Sally mimes different parts of the same task to each person. For example, if the task is clearing up after a meal, then Sally will mime carrying plates to her foster father, who will copy it and keep going. Sally will then mime drying up to her foster mother in the same way, and will then mime clearing the table to her foster sister. Everyone keeps their part of the mime going, while guessing what they are doing as a family, matching their description as closely as possible to the words on the list.

After the family have guessed the task, they then move on to the next item on the list, with a different family member teaching the individual mimes. If possible, make sure everyone has a turn. It is good to congratulate the family on the way they are all working together as they do this task.

The second part of the activity is to brainstorm ways in which the family work together already, and how they would like to work together in the future. Label the categories on a large piece of paper as 'We are a team' and 'We will be a team'. At this point you may wish to include some of the areas where all can work towards a common goal, even if not on the same task, as indicated in the first paragraph under 'Method' above.

The second list is very useful for you to have some aims for your work with the family.

SEE ALSO

- Family Escape Routes (CT1, p.92)

The Three Rs: Roles, Responsibilities, Rights
(Age: 9 years and upwards)

Aim

To help children see that they have a role, responsibilities and rights within their family and that as they get older these will change and increase. This can also help indirectly to strengthen their identity and highlight their importance in their family.

Materials

Paper and pencils, colouring pens.

Method

Explain to the child that in life we all have roles such as being a son or foster son; we all have responsibilities such as things we have to do, e.g. feed the pets; and we all have rights such as the right to go and play with friends. Explain that as you grow up these three Rs increase and change. For example, if they have older siblings or foster brothers and sisters they may have different roles and more responsibilities and rights. This means that they can make more decisions about their life.

Divide the page into three columns and label each column 'Roles', 'Responsibilities' and 'Rights'. If the child does not understand these descriptions, change them to easier ones such as 'Who I am', 'What I have to do', 'Special things I am allowed to do'.

Down the side of the page write a yearly time scale starting from their current age. As you fill in the chart you will probably need to give plenty of prompts, especially for the younger child. To help think about how the three Rs change as they get older they could think about their older sibling and foster children, if they have them. Once written, review it with the child.

As can be seen in figure 3.2, this 12-year-old was able to see that she would have increasing rights to decide whether she saw her birth mum more frequently and eventually whether she wanted to live with her birth mother.

See also

- I'll Get There Someday (p. 108)
- Future Profile (CT1, p.95)

- You do not get to watch TV tomorrow night, miss a turn!
- You are grounded, go back 2 spaces.

The cards should then be placed in a pile on the game board.

To play the game

Using counters or small objects and a dice, play 'Pick Up a Privilege' as follows. The first player throws the dice and moves the appropriate number of squares. If the player lands on a P or a C, they pick up a corresponding card and follow the instructions on it. The next player does the same, until one player reaches the final square labelled 'You've Won' or 'Finish'.

Remember to praise the child for the way he or she has behaved while making and playing the game. Complete your time with the child by finding out what type of privileges and responsibilities the child may want and when the child thinks that he or she will be likely to get them. Share this information with the carers and encourage its incorporation in any reward system they are using.

SEE ALSO

- Shuddering Snakes and Likeable Ladders (CT1, p.73)

Figure 3.3 Pick up a Privilege

Chapter 4

Understanding Relationships

As indicated in chapter 1, forming positive attachments is extremely important for a child who has moved between families. Yet this is not easy, especially when the child is over-friendly with everyone or never friendly with anyone. There will also be a different emphasis on promoting a strong attachment, depending on the permanency and nature of the placement. It can be difficult and confusing for the adults involved, but it is likely to be even less clear for the child. Often the child has a very poor understanding of relationships and cannot discriminate between safe people and those likely to bring him or her harm. Therefore, you will see some overlap in the aims of the activities in this chapter, and often they can be used to help in child protection and/or to help build good relationships with the significant people now in their lives.

Near and Far (Age: 8 –14 years)

AIM

To gain insight into how children view the significant adults in their lives.

MATERIALS

A4 paper, small easily peelable note stickers, a photocopier, pens.

METHOD

This activity provides a good opportunity to encourage the child to have the confidence to be honest about his or her feelings.

Draw a series of evenly spaced circles, as in figure 4.1. However, we recommend that the smallest circle is about 5 cm in diameter and the largest about 18 cm. Four circles are usually enough. In the middle, encourage the child to draw the outline of a heart, a flower, a car or anything else that he or she wants to. The child's name then should be written in the middle of this shape. Explain that this diagram is going to help you find out who they feel close to and who is important to them now, and how they think this may change in the future.

To do this, ask the child to write down the names of the important people in his or her life on the small post-it notes. Then ask the child to place the post-it notes on the diagram with those that he or she feels closest to next to their shape, then those who are not so close in the next circle, and so on. Discuss with the child the reasons for putting people in certain positions. Then photocopy this piece of work and take the post-it notes off. Explain that this time they are going to place the people where they wish they were or, alternatively, you could ask them to place them where they think they will be by the time they are grown up. This can lead into a valuable discussion about how the children feel about their relationships, how they may like them to change and how long they think they will last.

Be prepared for the child to make some discoveries while doing this activity, because it allows him or her to stand back and view the situation from a different angle. For example, they may discover that they feel stronger towards their foster carers than their stepfather. Help them to understand that they can love more than one person at a time, and that their feelings towards others in their life can be very complex.

Note that the second part of this activity is not recommended when the plan is for the child to move on or where the foster carers state clearly that their involvement will end when the child is 16 years old.

SEE ALSO

- Family Feelings (p. 56)

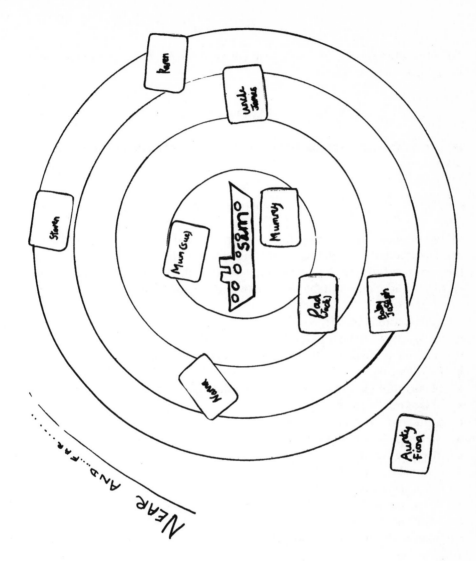

Figure 4.1   Near and Far

Friend or Foe (Age: 6 years and upwards)

AIM

To help children learn to distinguish between the people they can trust and the people they cannot.

MATERIALS

Prepared cards, three prepared boxes (see box template instructions, Appendix 1).

METHOD

Make your boxes and cards prior to starting the activity. Your prepared cards need to be small enough to slide through the slots in the boxes. The items on the card need to reflect a wide range of attributes or ways of behaving towards a child. Some suitable items may include the following:

- Makes sure I am safe
- Makes sure I have my dinner/lunch money
- Asks me to do things that make me feel uncomfortable
- Frightens me
- Makes sure I know where they are if they go away
- Makes me feel safe
- Is pleased when I am happy
- Makes me feel better if I am sad
- Buys me sweets
- Cares about how I feel
- Gives me money
- Wants me with them when they are on their own
- Wants me to keep bad secrets
- Likes to give me happy surprises
- Hurts me
- Teaches me how to look after myself

Try to avoid 'loves me' and 'hates me' if the child has been abused in the past. It may well have been by someone who loves them, or who they believe loves them. Obviously, dealing with this issue can be very sensitive and may be beyond the scope of this activity.

Discuss with the child how some people are our friends and care about what happens to us, whereas others are definitely not on our side. Use your knowledge of the child to illustrate this to him or her. For example, if the child is being bullied at school this would provide an example of someone who does not want the best for him or her.

Take the three prepared boxes and use the child's own language to label one as foe, one as friend and the third as 'don't know'. The third box is vital in this activity because it reflects true life that someone who is behaving in a certain way will not necessarily be a friend. Work through your prepared cards, letting the child slot them in where he or she feels is appropriate. However, this activity is mostly about providing a vehicle for discussion with the child. You may need to stress that it is not a test with right or wrong answers, but a game to help the child talk about what the people around him or her are like.

Note that this activity may not be suitable where children have such strong loyalty to a previous abuser that they are not yet ready to accept that they were not safe. Use other activities, such as The Safety Net, first.

The Safety Net (Age: 7–14 years)

AIM

To help children identify the people in their lives who will keep them safe.

MATERIALS

A4 paper, colouring pens, net from fruit bags or similar (optional), glue and spare paper of various colours.

METHOD

Talk to the children about any time in their lives when they have not felt safe. Discuss how there are times in everyone's life when we need to know which people are able to provide a safe place or where to go to keep out of danger. If you have already used an activity like Near and Far (p. 31), then refer to this list of people. Discuss with the child which ones would keep him or her safe, not just in an emergency but on a day-to-day basis. Children may already have some understanding of how some people have not kept them safe in the past and you may wish to draw on this if you can do so without detracting from the main aim of this activity. Also be careful here because you do not want to put the child in the position of being so scared of a previously abusive parent that the child does not want to keep the next contact arrangements.

As you have been discussing this you will probably want to introduce the activity. If you are using the actual net you may want to make a collage using the child's drawings of the people in his or her life who keep him or her safe.

The activity will be as illustrated in the figure 4.2. You may wish to introduce it by talking about trapeze artists or gymnasts and the need to have a safety net for them to land in. Encourage the child to choose the people who really will keep him or her safe to be the people holding the net either end. This is one instance where, if the child has done a picture, you may need to 'touch up' the drawing to ensure that the people who are keeping the child safe are actually holding the net! Let the child decide how to put him or herself in the net. In our illustration the child is shown falling from a great height, but it may be more relevant to depict the child as cradled by the net.

Finally, write or encourage the child to write a suitable caption to the picture, e.g. 'I know who can keep me safe'.

SEE ALSO

- Scared Sally and Brave Belinda (p. 70)

The People Puzzle (Age: 6 years and upwards)

AIM

This quiz is about the people and relationships in the child's life. It highlights which behaviours the child sees as appropriate for the different people in the child's life and what he or she expects from them. Therefore, it is useful to precede or complement any child protection work.

MATERIALS

Several sheets of A4 paper, pens.

METHOD

To do this activity you need to be fairly familiar with the people in the child's life. So this may be done better after you have seen the child for some sessions.

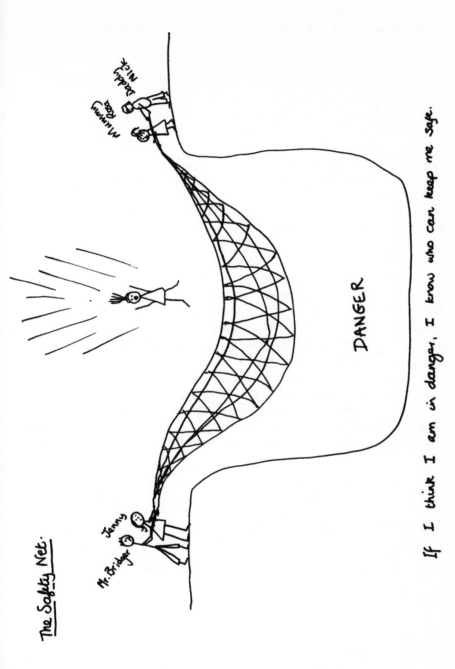

Figure 4.2 The Safety Net

The activity takes the form of a quiz, where you give clues to the child that help him or her to identify the correct person to answer the question, 'Who is it?' You need to have prepared some cards made from the A4 paper with a list of clues for the child to work through. Below is an example of some clues:

Who is it?

- You can give them a hug
- You can sit on their knee
- You can get in their car
- They can give you sweets
- They can walk past your house
- They can sell you a comic

You can also prepare a list of the people you have written clues about for the child to choose from. Include a stranger in your list of people, and people the child knows less well, e.g. the driver of the school bus. Of course some of the clues will fit more than one person. Discuss this with the child, and help the child if he or she has a skewed idea of relationships, e.g. if the child thinks it is appropriate to hug the stranger. Do not forget to record the child's initial answer in your own notes, so that you can use this game again after work on keeping safe, to see if the child's understanding of appropriate behaviours has changed.

Prepare a sheet for the child's folder, with a summary of appropriate information you have discussed from playing The People Puzzle, either in a simple list or, with an older child, in a table. For example:

	Mummy Jane	Dad	Granny	Joe	Sam	Mr P	Stranger
Good to give me a hug	Yes	Yes	Yes	Yes	No	No	No
OK to give me sweets	Yes	Yes	Yes	Yes	Yes	No	No
Can go to their house	Yes	No	Yes	No	No	No	No

SEE ALSO

- Torn to Shreds (p. 76)
- Safety Hand (CT1, p.70)
- Safety Soldier (CT1, p.87)

What Happens Next? (Age: 7 years and upwards)

Aim

This activity aims to explore with a child why others act in the way that they do. It also aims to give guidance as to some appropriate responses to others, highlighting to the child the consequences of his or her own actions.

Materials

Cards (approximately the size of playing cards), puppets, a container or hat.

Method

This activity can be a group role play or puppet activity.

You need to have made some cards in advance with scenarios on them that provide prompts for the child to consider 'what happens next?'. Below are some examples of possible scenarios but try to make your scenarios relevant to the child and his or her difficulties:

- Your teacher walks in just as you have pushed someone over.
- You are meant to be home at 7 o'clock and your friend tells you it is 7.30.
- You accidentally kick someone.
- Someone hits you for taking their ruler.
- Your foster mum tells you off and sends you to your room.
- Your social worker comes when you are watching your favourite TV programme.
- Your foster mum sees you hitting someone and calls you in, telling you that you are grounded.

Explain to the child that you are going to do an activity that looks at different situations that the child may find him or herself in and that together you are going to explore how to respond. The child then takes a card from the hat, with a scenario on it. You can then either:

- Discuss what happens next with the child and then act it out, with or with-out mime puppets, or
- The child mimes to you the scenario and you guess what the mime is. You then discuss what happens next and the child completes the mime with your agreed outcome. (However, for this option, all the situations written on the cards must be easy to act.)

Remember to help the child consider the consequences of his or her actions. If the child is not sure, spend time discussing the possible outcomes and how they could be avoided. After the child has come up with negative outcomes, repeat the activity after discussing what can be done to create more positive consequences. For example, there may be instances where the child could say sorry or do something to put things right.

It is useful to prepare a summary sheet to go in the child's folder, covering the main points about the consequences of their behaviour.

SEE ALSO

- Safety Hand (CT1, p.70)
- Escape Routes (CT1, p.90)
- Escape to Safety (CT1, p.92)

The Good Friends Game (Age: 6 years and upwards)

AIM

To help the child understand the qualities of friendship but that not every friend will have all these qualities.

MATERIALS

A3 prepared board (or the materials to make in the session), 24–30 blank cards around playing card size, five extra blank cards per player, dice and counters.

METHOD

To make the board

The board needs to be prepared as in figure 4.3. A simpler route can be made for younger children, but have a similar proportion of squares with Q or YES on them.

Making the cards

To begin with, talk to the child about what makes a good friend. Together, make some cards with the attributes of good friends written on them; make at least 11. Some examples are:

- Listens to me

- Shares her toys
- Asks me to play football with him
- Lets me borrow his pencil
- Asks me to play out
- Is mostly friendly towards me
- Makes up if we quarrel

On cards with these positive qualities write 'move on 3 ' or 'extra go' by the positive attribute.

Then talk to the child about what makes a person not such a good friend. Some of these can be the opposite of the positive attributes, but there may be some others you wish to include, such as:

- Bullies me
- Takes things out of my lunch box
- Gets me into trouble
- Makes me keep a bad secret
- Wants me to skip school

Write some cards with these negative qualities on them and by the side of the attributes write 'move back 3' or 'miss a go'.

Label all of these quality cards with a Q on the back. Prepare a further five cards per player with a child's face on each (perhaps cut from a magazine). Label these on the back as 'Good Friend'.

To play the game

The first player throws a dice and moves from the corner marked 'Start' in the direction indicated. If the player lands on a square with an arrow, the direction of the arrow has to be followed, depending on the direction he or she has come from. If the player lands on the middle square of the board, he or she may choose to go in any direction.

When a player lands on a 'Q' he or she picks up the top card from the qualities pile and if it is a positive card, the player obeys the instruction on it. However, if it is a negative card, it is passed to any other player who then obeys the instruction on it. If a player lands on a 'yes' he or she can take a 'Good Friend' card.

When a player has collected three positive qualities these can be swapped for one 'Good Friend' card from the pile. If a player has collected five negative quality cards then he or she has to put a 'Good Friend' card back on the pile. This cannot happen if the player has no 'Good Friend' cards. As you

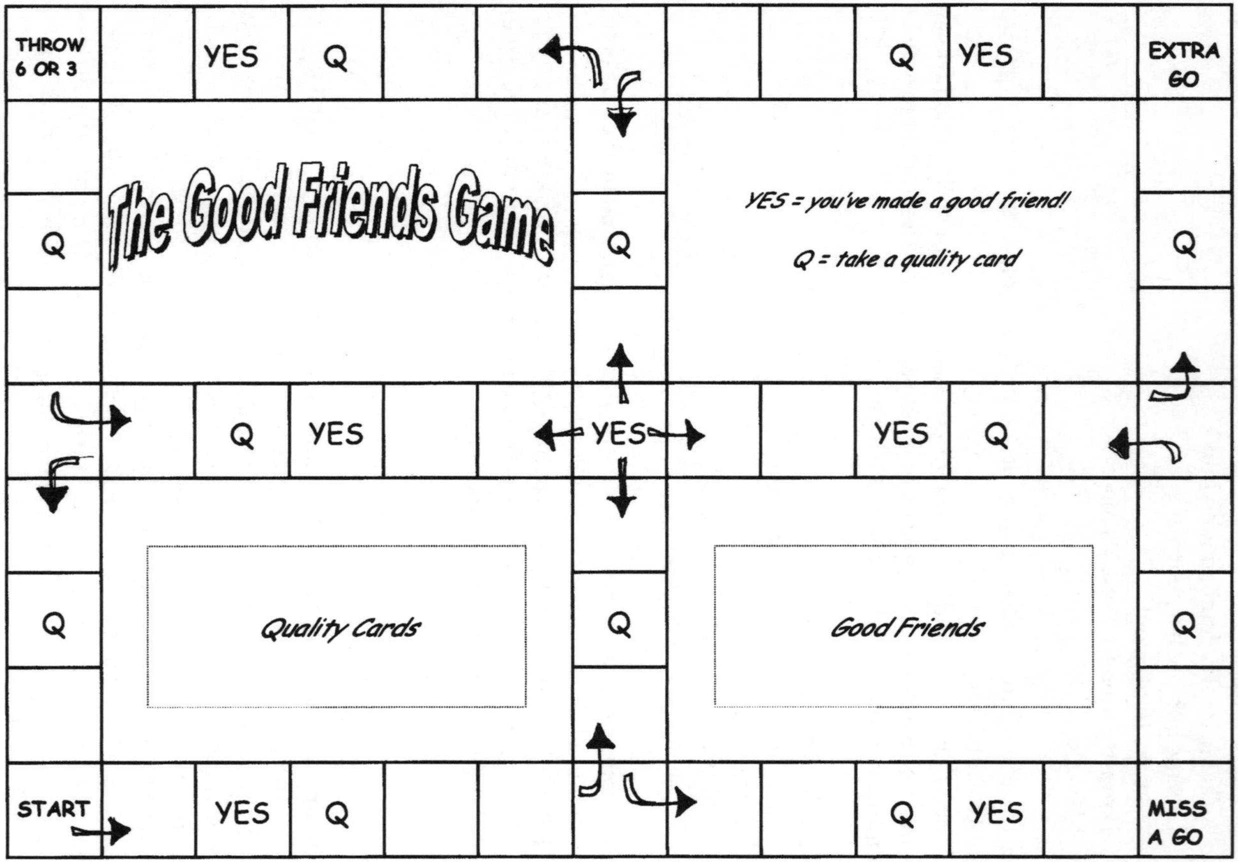

Figure 4.3 The Good Friends Game

play the game, be reading out the positive qualities each time they are picked up and again when someone earns a 'Good Friend'. It is even better if the child can be encouraged to read them out.

The winner is the person who has collected five good friends (or, if you want to make the game shorter, three).

As you finish the game, try to summarize the main ideas about friendship that may be pertinent to the child.

Variation: Making Good Friends

The game is essentially the same but, instead of writing qualities of good friends, write on the cards ways to make good friends, for example:

- Asking people how they are
- Asking them if they want to play
- Remembering their birthday
- Asking them to come to tea

The negative cards have statements that discourage friendships, for example:

- Shouting at them when they don't do as I say
- Being in charge all the time
- Telling them they are no good
- Not listening to them

Try to use the child's own ideas as long as they are appropriate. Discuss the ideas and help to develop them. As before, the positive statements are 'move on 3' or 'extra go' and the negative statements are 'move back 3' and 'miss a go'.

Chapter 5

Promoting Positive Identity

Children who have moved between families sometimes seem to have lost who they are along the way. Yet this sense of self is vital in helping the child be resilient and cope with adverse life circumstances. The activities in this chapter are designed to help children to build a positive self-image and be sure of themselves, building on their own strengths and skills.

Just Me (Age: 5 years and upwards)

AIM

This is a useful rapport-building exercise as well as an opportunity to get down on paper some of the child's likes, dislikes, strengths, skills and abilities.

MATERIALS

Strong A4 paper cut into two strips, lengthways. Sticky tape and colouring pens.

METHOD

Similar in content to our first activity 'Meet the Star', this is a very simple activity where the child makes a concertina-style booklet, perhaps with a drawing of him or herself or his or her name on the cover, with each folded section containing facts about the child.

To make the booklet, fold one strip in half, then half again, then use these guiding folds to concertina the strip. This gives four sections each side to be completed.

Use your knowledge of the child to begin to make suggestions about what could go into the 'Just Me' booklet. Encourage him or her by introducing a little humour, using words like 'My pet hates' or 'Things that bug me' and 'I am over the moon when'. It is best to put more positive items in the booklet than negative, so if the child is unable to think of good things, you may need to suggest some of the positive categories from the list below.

Involve the child as much as possible in making the booklet, only helping with the writing and drawing if the child is extremely reluctant to do it. The child may like to use little illustrations (see figure 5.1). Try to cram in as much information as possible, encircling items if you need to make the booklet clearer. If it looks as if you may not have enough space, concertina all or half of the second strip of paper and stick it on the end of the booklet. If the child cannot complete all the pages, suggest that the blank ones are for good ideas later.

As can be seen from figure 5.1, children can come up with some very interesting facts about themselves, which you can use later.

Possible suggestions are:

- The thing that bugs me most is . . .
- I love it when . . .
- My favourite colour is . . .
- It always makes me mad when . . .
- I was very, very, very excited when . . .
- I am proud as a peacock that I . . .
- My best time of the week is . . .
- The thing I like best about my looks is . . .
- People think I am cool when . . .
- I am so ashamed that I wish the floor would swallow me up when . . .
- My best bit of work was . . .
- Happiness to me is . . .
- I believe in . . .
- My favourite animal is . . .
- One thing I can always eat is . . .
- If I am upset I . . .
- I am over the moon when . . .
- I always get the giggles when . . .

When the booklet is finished, discuss anything the child found difficult. Try to finish on a positive note by referring back to the positives or funny items. The booklet can be taken home and is ideal for standing on a shelf or mantelpiece for display.

SEE ALSO

- Meet the Star (p. 7)
- My world (CT1, p.11)
- I am . . . (CT1, p.11)

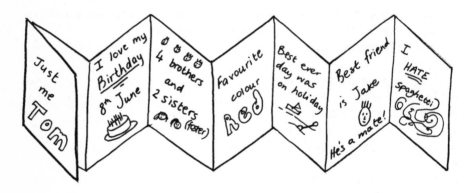

Figure 5.1   Just Me

The Loveable Me (Age: 8–14 years)

To help the child find likeable qualities about themselves, in a lighthearted atmosphere.

A4 paper, colouring pens.

It is best if you have thought this activity through before you use it with the child, so that you can have some ideas if the child is stuck.

Introduce the idea of an acronym, and if the child is not familiar with it then explain what it is, perhaps by using slightly humourous ones such as SWALK (Sealed With A Loving Kiss). Explain to the child that you are going to make one for them, using the phrase 'Loveable . . .', with the child's name. If the child thinks 'loveable' is silly, change it to 'likeable or 'special'. Try to use appropriate phrases for the child, and if the child comes up with something that is very untrue, put the truth in brackets afterwards, with the word 'actually' or just 'he wishes!!'. It does not matter if you cheat slightly, by writing the word around the target letter. An example acronym for a 14-year-old is given below, but yours obviously will be tailored to the child and his or her positive (or neutral) attributes, likes and wishes:

Long-legged Beth
Other children like her
Very often she is top of her class at music
Every day she remembers to clean her room (we wish!!)
Angela, her mum, loves her
Boys think she's gorgeous
Little bothers her
Egg and chips is one of her favourite meals

Beth wants a dog
Even a little one
The best holiday she ever had was in Cyprus
Happiness for her is a day off from school.

Depending on the age of the child, the acronym can be illustrated. Use the piece of work to help the child build up a positive view of him or herself. This piece of work is for display and the example by a 10-year-old child (figure 5.2) is well worthy of a place of honour where everyone can see it at home. If there are other siblings, or foster siblings, it may be appropriate to encourage the carer to make acronyms with them as well.

SEE ALSO

- Today's Star Guest (p. 10)
- Meet the Star (p. 7)
- Good Things about Me (CT1, p.119)
- Best Achievements (CT1, p.127)

Handfuls of Happiness (Age: 6–14 years)

AIM

To help the child focus on happy thoughts, feelings and memories.

MATERIALS

A4 paper, colouring pens, stars.

METHOD

This very simple activity can be done while talking to the child more deeply about the happy thoughts, feelings and memories you are recording. However, it must be used sensitively, perhaps in sessions after you have already helped the child to understand that you are listening to his or her very real fears and concerns. Otherwise, the child may feel that you are glossing over issues that he or she wishes to address.

Explain to the child that the title of the piece of work is 'Handfuls of Happiness' and that today you will together think of as many happy things as possible, to fill up a picture. You may wish to put this in context with the other work you have done. The activity is slightly different, depending upon the age group.

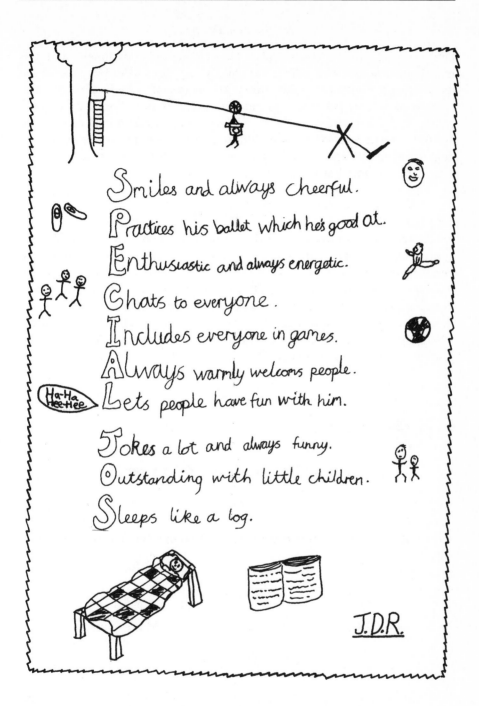

Figure 5.2   Special Me

For the younger child

Draw round his or her hands. Talk to the child about happy times using cues like 'Your best day ever'. Write the child's responses from the palm of the hand up each finger, using the thumbs last, in case the child's concentration has waned by then. Add pictures and stars as appropriate. For example, if the child says 'When I did my best work at school', a star definitely needs to be added by the picture. With some children you will need to use this exercise to help in the understanding of happiness, using phrases like 'when you felt all warm and comfortable and good inside'.

For the older child

Encourage the child to draw, or draw yourself, some open hands, slightly cupped with wrists together (see figure 5.3). You may need to hold your own hands in that position as a model for the child to draw them. Draw a few 'bubbles' in the hand and start to fill with happy thoughts, etc. and add more as the child proceeds, remarking on how many (but not how few!) there are. Be very encouraging and suggest times when people sometimes feel happy. Also include any happy wishes for the future, e.g. 'When I think about myself grown-up and living in my own flat'.

SEE ALSO

- Meet the Star (p. 7)

Snappy Choices (Age: 7–13 years)

AIM

To provide a gentle introduction to the idea that the child's views are important.

MATERIALS

Two sheets of A4 paper, pens, separate paper to record responses.

METHOD

You may wish to prepare two snappers before the session, or make them with the child, depending on level of ability.

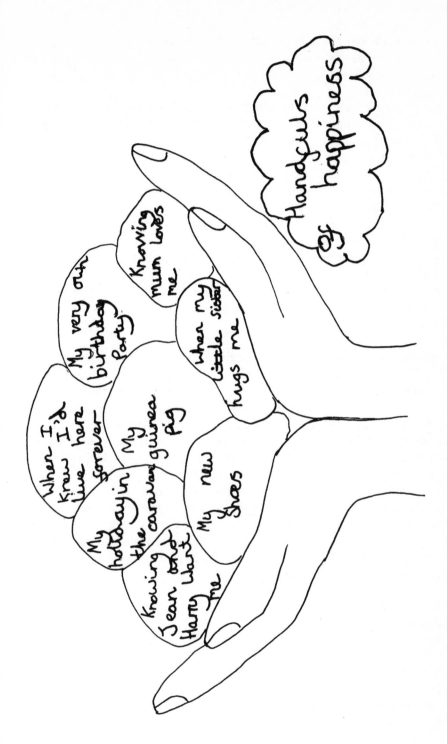

Figure 5.3 Handfuls of Happiness

Snappers are simple paper sculptures that can be opened to reveal questions or statements. 'Snapper' is our name for them, because among all our friends who have used them in the playground in their youth, none can remember their name!

If you have not come across them before, the illustration (figure 5.4) may help you to understand what it is you are trying to reproduce! However, our instructions are tried and tested and not nearly as complicated as they first look.

To make the snapper:

- Take a square of paper, the largest you can make with an A4 sheet
- Find the mid-point, then fold all corners in to the mid-point
- Turn the sheet over and fold the new corners in, in the same way
- Turn the snapper over
- Turn each of the corners touching the mid-point up to their respective corners of the square. Now comes the tricky bit!
- Put your thumb and forefinger of one hand under two adjacent triangle corners, and do the same with your other hand under the other two (your thumbs should be adjacent)

To operate the snapper, put your thumbs together and your forefingers together. Now practise putting them apart and back together and then pulling the corners sideways with your forefingers and thumbs together. Always pass through the point where all your fingers are together (the mid-point pass).

To turn the snapper into a therapeutic tool, you will need to use it to ask questions about the child. So under every flap there needs to be a question. Number your covering flaps (the ones on the outside of where your thumbs and forefingers go) with a simple 1, 2, 3, 4. Under each of the four flaps will be a question about favourites, e.g. 'What is your favourite colour/food/animal/song?'.

On the other side (which is the inside) you will see eight triangles. Write the numbers 5 to 12 on these triangles. Under the flap for each of these numbers you will be able to write further questions for the child to answer. Keep these simple for a younger child, but they can be more complicated for those over 10 years old. Some examples are:

- Best day of the week
- Best friend
- Worst homework
- Something you really hate
- Best place to go
- Favourite person
- Something you are good at
- Best subject at school

- Worst subject at school

To play the game, ask the child to choose a number from the first four. Lift the flap and ask him or her the question. You can then use the snapper by making a mid-point pass for each letter of the child's answer (e.g. 'blue' would need four mid-point passes). You will then have four numbers showing inside the snapper. Let the child choose one and then move the snapper according to the number chosen. Let the child choose a number again, and this time lift the flap and read out the question.

This all sounds as if it will take a long time, but in fact it is very quick. The child is usually quite eager to take a turn, or use or make their own snapper. Keep the game going until most questions are covered – if you want to gain information about the child more quickly you may need to say 'I don't know, how would you answer that?' when the child is asking you. If the child can cope with a fairly slow pace, write down the answers as you go, ready for a poster or decorated list of all the important things you have found out.

Make sure the child takes the snapper home, then it is likely to be used between sessions, helping the child to gain attention in a positive way. If snappers are not already known among the child's peers, it will provide a good vehicle for the child to make positive relationships as friends are taught how to make one.

Variation: Family Choices (Age: 7 years and upwards)

Snappers are quite good fun to make with a whole family, and will provide a lot of information for an incoming child about other family members, and

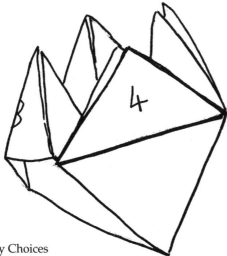

Figure 5.4   Snappy Choices

vice versa.

Use in exactly the same way, but the adults may wish to make up their own questions. Encourage them not to focus on the past and emotive issues, but on getting to know the child and promoting a positive identity.

Again, make sure they go home with each family member and encourage them to use them at home.

SEE ALSO

- Today's Star Guest (p. 10)
- Connecting Questions (p. 11)
- Telling Trivia (p. 12)
- I Believe (CT1, p.124)
- Best Achievements (CT1, p.127)
- Good Things about Me (CT1, p.119)
- Sentence Completion (CT1, p.16)

Chapter 6

Understanding Feelings

The expression of feelings may be all too easy for a child who has moved between families, or it may be extremely difficult. The task of the therapist will be to help the child to direct anger or sadness appropriately and then move on to more positive feelings. Not all of the following activities will suit every child. For example, children who cannot yet externalize feelings will need to learn first of all to recognize that they do have feelings. On the other hand, children who direct feelings at the wrong person will need to learn that it is acceptable to feel angry or sad, but that these feelings need to be channelled appropriately, so that they do not negatively affect their present lives.

The Feelings Spinning Wheel
(Age: 5 years and upwards)

Aim

To help children start to talk about feelings and to discuss how these relate to events and their own circumstances. It also helps to give the younger child an emotional vocabulary.

Materials

Colouring pens, thin card approximately 16 cm × 16 cm, a cocktail stick, ruler, scissors.

METHOD

On the card use the ruler to draw a hexagon shape (see figure 6.1) and cut this out. Draw lines to divide the hexagon into six sections. Explain to the child that you are going to make a feelings spinning wheel to play a game with. Label each section with a feeling, making sure that you cover both negative and positive feelings. Encourage the child to think of the feelings him or herself. For a younger child you may need to write down only a few feelings so you could label sections twice and illustrate with the aid of faces with smiles, tears, etc.

Pierce the hexagon in the centre and put the cocktail stick through the hole; it should fit very tightly. You now have a feelings wheel that can be spun and will land on one of its sides. The side it lands on indicates the emotion under discussion.

Explain that each player gets a point for thinking about a time when he or she felt the way that is indicated by the spinning wheel.

Obviously as the therapist you need to use discretion when talking about your own feelings, so do not make it personal. Tailor your response so that it is relevant to the child. Some children are quite happy to use your 'go' to talk about their own feelings. You could issue double points if the child talks about feelings that he or she has not actually spun.

Always end this activity by reverting to discussing a positive feeling, with or without the aid of the feelings spinning wheel.

Variation: Family Feelings

This could be played with a family to help them begin to feel comfortable about talking about feelings together. To begin with they could choose situations that are not too close and then move on to talk more about their difficulties. Encourage all members of the family to take part.

This activity also could be useful to draw in feelings that arise because of another family member's actions, so that they can be discussed openly. Make sure the family are guided to some positive ways of changing how they relate to each other for the better.

SEE ALSO

- Handfuls of Happiness (p. 48)
- Mood Scales (CT1, p.24)
- Happy, Sad, Angry (CT1, p.17)
- Feelwheel (CT1, p.25)

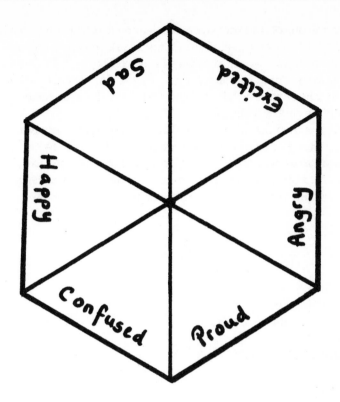

Figure 6.1   The Fellings Spinning Wheel

Strings of Feelings (Age: 9 years and upwards)

AIM

To help generate feelings with a child. This activity can be used as the first step to understanding how a child feels.

MATERIALS

A4 paper, colouring pens and highlighter pen (optional).

METHOD

Explain to the child that you are going to brainstorm as many feelings as you can both think of, ready to make a 'string of feelings' by linking one feeling to another using one of the letters from one feeling to start the next feeling word. Alternatively the young person may want to take it across the last one. Both variations are shown in our examples (figure 6.2).

When you have both run out of ideas, ask the child to circle or highlight the feelings that he or she has felt over the past week. This can facilitate a discussion about the child's feelings.

The work is then useful as a visual aid, to talk about how one feeling can lead to another. For example, if we are feeling tired and fed up then this is likely to lead to us being snappy and irritable if we are asked to help wash up. See if the child can give examples from his or her own experience.

Try to end the session by talking about when the child has a really good feeling.

See also

- Love Grows (p. 79)
- Overflowing Love (p. 80)
- Boxful of Feelings (CT1, p.28)
- Feelings Pie (CT1, p.26)
- Wordsearch (CT1, p.79)

Feelings Basket (Age: 5–10 years)

Aim

To help the child feel relaxed with you by working on a short craft task, before using the product to introduce the idea of talking about feelings.

Materials

For each basket – two sheets of strong paper, colouring pens, scissors, glue stick or sticky tape. For the feelings cards – two sheets of A4 paper, scissors, colouring pens, star stickers (optional).

Method

Talk to the child about how you are going to make a basket out of paper ready for a game about how we think and feel.

The basket to be made is very simple in design, so that it can be put to-

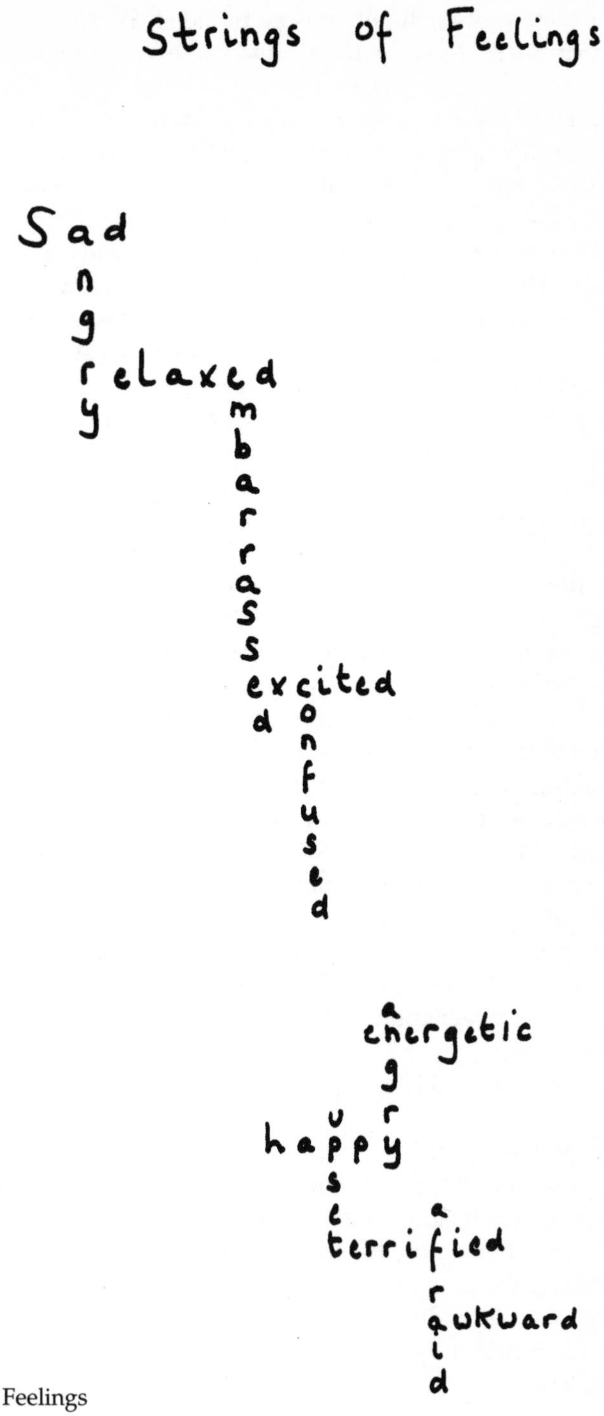

Strings of Feelings

Sad
angry
relaxed
embarrassed
excited
confused

energetic
angry
happy
used
terrified
afraid
awkward

Figure 6.2 Strings of Feelings

gether quite quickly to allow time to use it. With older children, you may wish to make a basket while the child makes one, thus demonstrating how to do it as you go along.

Take one A4 sheet. Fold 2 cm in down each of the long sides (see figure 6.3). Find the midway point by folding lightly in half, matching the top of the A4 sheet to the bottom. Then make two proper folds inwards, 1.5 cm either side of the midway point. This forms the base. Cut in 2 cm along the fold each side. Fold the basket into shape. You are now ready to glue or tape together the sides, being careful to make them fit in such a way that the base is kept flat. (You may find it easier to put a suitably sized book into the basket to keep it in shape while you stick it. If you are using sticky tape, it helps to have small lengths prepared rather than trying to use long strips.) Before glueing the flaps at the side of the base, you may wish to snip off the corners for neatness.

The handle is made by cutting a width of A4, approximately 4 cm wide, folding and sticking it in half lengthways and then sticking each end onto the basket.

The thin card is used to make the feelings cards that go in the basket. For younger children you may wish to have the cards ready prepared, or at least cut up ready for use. The cards can be any shape, as long as there is room to write a feeling on each card and, for a younger child, to draw a face depicting the feeling. Usually six or eight cards will be sufficient, and an even number is best if you are using the activity with the child and taking turns. While you are making the cards together, it is a good time to start talking about feelings and when the child feels happy, sad, scared or whatever other emotion is on the card. Make sure you include the child in the making of the cards in some way, e.g. a very young child may enjoy putting star stickers on the back while you are doing the writing.

The game involves pulling cards out of the basket. The person with the card does not show it to the other player but mimes (or acts) the feeling on the card. For a younger child, this may be by making the same face that is on the card. The other player has to guess the feeling that is being acted. Take it in turns to do this, again talking about when the child feels that way at each point.

Then talk to the child about how we sometimes carry our feelings with us all the time and they get all mixed up just how they are in the basket. Ask the children which feelings they would like to have with them all the time and which ones they do not like having. Discuss with them whether they would like to leave the unwanted feelings with you, so that you can talk about those feelings next time they come. Before you finish the session, make sure the child has opportunity to describe something that will give him or her a positive feeling.

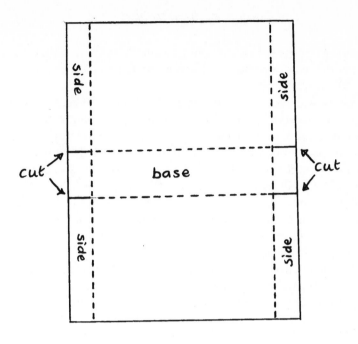

Figure 6.3   Feelings Basket

Variation: Feelings Wallet

Some children may prefer to make a feelings wallet. To make a wallet, cut just over a third off the lengths of the A4 sheets to make two pieces of paper approximately 19 cm × 21 cm.

Take one of these pieces of paper and fold it 1.5 cm off-centre (shortest length across) and the second sheet likewise but 3 cm off-centre. Sticky tape or glue the short edges of the first sheet together, then slip it inside the second sheet to form the pockets of the wallet (see figure 6.4). Stick the outside edges of both together. Fold the wallet in half. A small piece of sticky tape or glue down the centre fold will divide the wallet to form eight pockets for the feelings cards, which can be made as in the instructions for the feelings basket. You will need to ensure that the cards are the right size to fit the wallet. Encourage the child to decorate the wallet.

Play the game as for the feelings basket.

If the children do not like you keeping the negative feelings because it leaves the wallet rather empty, provide some blank cards asking them to prepare some more positive feelings for you, ready for the next session.

See also

- A pocketful of feelings (CT1, p.28)

Flying Fears (Age: 6–12 years)

Aim

To introduce the idea that fears and worries can go away.

Materials

Several sheets of A4 paper, colouring pens, wastepaper bin (optional).

Method

Make several paper aeroplanes with the child (see paper plane instructions, Appendix 2), but do not let him or her fly them yet! Have several planes for the child and perhaps one or two for you so that you can join in. Explain to the child that these planes are going to have all his or her fears and worries

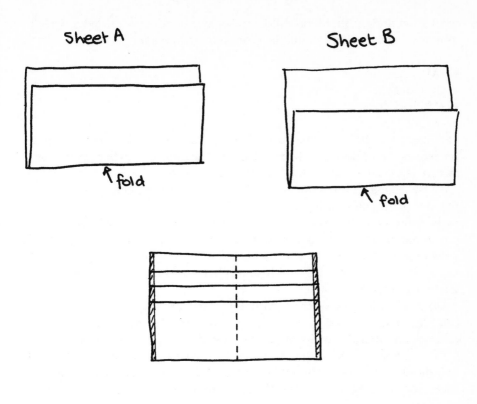

Figure 6.4 Feelings Wallet

written on them. Talk to the child, or use your previous knowledge, to help him or her decide what should be written on each plane. For example:

● Monsters
● The dark
● My bad dream

On your own planes, write simply 'Flying Fears'. Once the writing is done, the planes can be flown. Talk to the child all the time you do this about how it is he or she who is making the fears fly away, so he or she is in control. If you have a wastepaper bin in the room, the metaphor can be enlarged to include the idea of the fears ending up as unwanted rubbish, as you both aim to land your planes in the bin. When the child retrieves the plane after flying it away, talk about how even if a fear returns the child can get rid of it again. If you have to show the child how to fly the plane more successfully (or the child has to show you!), use this to illustrate that working together is important when making fears fly away.

Go on to explain to the child about how there are ways in which he or she can learn to reduce and manage fears and worries (see other activities in this chapter) and that you will work on this together in a future session.

Try to persuade the child to leave the Flying Fear planes behind with you, to indicate that fears can be left behind. In order to be successful in this, you may need to make some other planes (without writing on) for the child to decorate at home.

See also

● Worry Box (CT1, p.54)

After You (Age: 7–13 years)

Aim

To introduce the idea that we can work to diminish a child's fear. This is especially useful when a child is having nightmares and flashbacks. Alternatively, this activity can be used solely as a rapport-building exercise.

Materials

Two sheets of A4 paper, colouring pens.

Both you and the child take a piece of paper – it may be best and easier if you have already pre-folded it, as in figure 6.5. It is not important how many sections you have, although if you are using our guidance you will need six.

You will see from figure 6.5 that each piece of paper is 'rolled over' as you proceed through this activity.

Explain to the child that you will be drawing a monster between you. First you will each draw the top of a monster's head (without letting each other see what you are doing). You need to ensure that your drawing of the head is to the edge of the page and a little beyond, so that when you swap pictures you can see where to continue with the drawing. The next section of the paper will have the bottom half of the head. Then you will continue in the same way, swapping between sections to make your monster. When completed, open it out together and point out how funny the monster looks!

A suggested sequence of monster segments could be:

- Top of head
- Rest of head
- Top half of body (including arms, if the monster has some!)
- Rest of body
- Top half of legs
- Rest of legs and feet (and tail if the monster has one)

Talk to the child about how, when we get frightening thoughts in our minds, we can share them with someone, just like we have shared drawing a picture of a monster. This will help break up the fear and together you can work on it.

Depending on your knowledge of the child's needs, this activity could be a good preamble to other activities such as ' Flying Fears' (p. 62) or 'Grumbling Gertie and Merry Maud' (p. 67).

SEE ALSO

- The Pit (CT1, p. 49)
- Worry Box (CT1, p. 54)

Figure 6.5   After You

Grumbling Gertie and Merry Maud (Grumbling George and Merry Mike) (Age: 7 years and upwards)

AIM

To encourage children who think negatively to begin to work on thoughts and positive self-statements.

MATERIALS

30 (or 31) rectangles of thin card (approximately playing card size), pens, paper for scoresheet.

METHOD

Explain to the child that you are going to be making a game that concentrates on the ways we think. Use your knowledge of the child to begin to write some of the GG (Grumbling Gertie or Grumbling George) statements on the front of the cards. Write nothing on the back of any of the cards. Write on the playing cards in the portrait orientation (i.e. short sides to the top and bottom).

Explain that the GG cards have not got to contain all grumbling thoughts, but could include any worries or upsetting thoughts. The types of negative thoughts we have from children vary from 'Nobody really cares about me' to 'I'm worried about leaving the cats when we go on holiday'. Use ten of the cards to write down negative statements. If the child runs out of ideas, make sure you say how good that is, but say you need a few more for the game and add in some that are perhaps similar to those the child has expressed to you in previous sessions. Number each of these cards consecutively. Label them GG in the top left and bottom right corners.

Together with the child prepare two MM cards for each GG card. The MM cards (Merry Mauds or Merry Mikes) are positive statements that counteract the negative ones. For example, if the child's GG is 'I am afraid of the dark' then the MM cards could be: 'Mum lets me have the table lamp on and that makes me feel better' and 'I know there is nothing to be afraid of really'. Number each of the MM cards that go with the GG with the same number as the GG, so that the complete set is identifiable, but put MM in the corner (see figure 6.6).

Do this for all the statements, so that you end up with ten sets, each with one GG and two MM cards (30 cards in total).

Talk about the statement on each GG card in turn. Help the child put a large X through the negative statement on the GG. Then cover the GG card over with the two appropriate MM cards. Explain how the positive thoughts can help get rid of the negative ones.

There are two ways to play the game:

- *Memory game*. The quick, simple game is a memory game, where the cards are shuffled, spread out face down and you and the child take turns to turn over three at a time. When either of you turn over a complete set, that set of cards has been 'won' by that player and is put aside. Whoever wins the set, reads out the positive cards. The winner is the person who collects the most sets.
- *Smart thinking*. For older children, the second, noisy game requires three players, so you may need to bring the carer into the session. The game also requires an extra card that says 'Wobbly Thought, lose 10'. All the cards are shuffled and then dealt. This means that one player has an extra card, but this varies as the dealer changes for each round. The players look at the cards in their hands and sort them into numbered sets as far as possible, without the other players seeing. One GG and two MM cards, with matching numbers make one set. If the child cannot manage to hold the cards, find a piece of card or books to use as barriers for all the players.

  The aim of the game is to collect sets of cards and to get rid of the Wobbly Thought and any unwanted GG cards because they will both lose points.

  A round starts by the dealer shouting 'Start Thinking'. Then 'Change'. On the word 'Change' the players pass two 'unwanted' cards to their right. Giving only enough time for the slowest player to take stock, the dealer shouts 'Change' again. Again two cards are passed to the right. If the game begins to get stuck with the same cards going round, the dealer can shout 'Change Card' and at least one of the cards that each player is passing round must be substituted for another from that player's hand.

  As each player collects a set, they put their completed set down on the table in front of them.

  The first player to have three complete sets slams them down on the table, shouting 'Smart Thinking'. This player scores 50 points, the others have 10 taken off for the Wobbly Thought, 5 taken off for each GG and 5 added on for each MM.

  If time allows, play six rounds of the game, i.e. let each player be the dealer twice.

For either game, encourage the child to take the game home to play, priming the carer to discuss the thoughts on the cards each time the game is played.

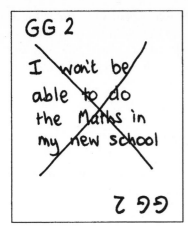

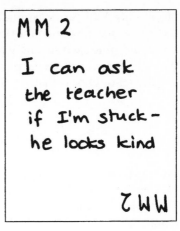

Figure 6.6 Grumbling Gertie and Merry Maud

Variation 1: Speedy Merry Mike (Speedy Merry Maud)

For younger children, start with three or four sets and work up. You keep the
GG cards and the child has the MM cards. You pick at random a GG card and
read it out. The child (using the MM cards to help) shouts back the statements

on the two MM cards as quickly as possible. You could set a timer for 30 seconds to see how often the child can remember both MM cards speedily, or you could time each set and watch the time 'record' get faster. This will help the child to have automatic positive thoughts, which will hopefully interrupt negative thoughts as they begin.

Variation 2: GG-ruMMy

The cards can be used to play a form of rummy. This works best if you make two extra MM cards that have MM+ in the corners. On the cards, write 'Extra Positive Thought'. You also need another Wobbly Thought card for this game.

For two players, deal six cards each and put the remaining ones in a pile. Turn the top card over next to it, to form two piles. The aim of the game is to put down two complete sets of cards. The MM+ card can be substituted for any MM card.

Each player completes a turn by picking up a card from either pile and either chooses to keep it or puts it down face up on the already facing up pile. If the player keeps it, then he or she must select another one from his or her hand to put down on the facing up pile. Obviously players will not wish to keep the Wobbly Thought cards, because they will lose 10 points if they still have them in their hand at the end of the round.

When someone has completed two sets, they have won the round and score 50 points. The loser still gains 5 points for each MM they have and 10 for an MM+, but loses 5 for any GG and loses 10 for a Wobbly Thought.

Every time a winner has used an MM+ card, encourage him or her to think of a very positive thought before writing down the score! While scores are being written down it is a good time to refer to the thoughts on the cards, and emphasize the need to remember the positive thoughts.

Variation 3: Scared Sally and Brave Belinda
(Scared Sam and Brave Billy)

The same game can be tailored to work specifically on feelings of anxiety. This can be general anxiety or for a specific incident. For example, we have found it useful when children have needed to tell a secret that an adult has asked them to keep. Helping children to understand that they have done well to overcome their fear and bravely tell the secret has helped them to resolve the guilt and torn feelings.

- Clear Thinking (CT1, p.84)
- Self-talk (CT1, p.93)

Catching my Anger (Age: 7 years and upwards)

AIM

To help children recognize the signs and triggers to their anger, so that they can learn to control it.

MATERIALS

A4 paper and pens.

METHOD

Draw a large net on the page; this could be a butterfly net or a fishing net, or whatever the child suggests. Begin to discuss with the children that in order to help them with their anger you first need to work out what the signs are that show they are getting angry and the possible triggers. Together you are going to work these out and catch them in your net.

Help the children think about what makes them angry and then focus on both the physical signs of anger (getting hot, shaky, feeling tense) and (if they can) what thoughts are going through their minds, as these can be an important part of treating anger. Display all the signs and the triggers that you have identified in the net, as shown in figure 6.7.

Explain to the children that in the same way as you have drawn the signs of anger in the net, so it is important that they catch the signs of anger. In this way, they will know they are getting angry and together you may find ways to stop their bad temper. You could then encourage the children to record their anger in the next week, maybe by ticking any of the items in the net that have occurred.

An older child may prefer to do this activity without drawing a net, but simply making a list of physical signs of anger and triggers.

SEE ALSO

- Target Practice (p. 92)
- Test and Try (p. 94)
- What Happened Next? (p. 38)
- Reasons Why (CT1, p. 19)
- Mood Scales (CT1, p. 24)
- Costs and Benefits (CT1, p. 51)

The Anger Debugging Kit (Age: 7–13 years)

AIM

To help generate some strategies for children to use in order to control their temper.

MATERIALS

A4 paper, pens and pencils.

METHOD

Talk to the children about how you are going to help them find ways to control their temper. Together you are going to make an anger debugging kit with all the strategies that will help them know what do to.

To engender enthusiasm you could suggest to the child that he or she could pretend to be a special agent – whose mission it is to use the kit to defeat his or her anger. Remind him or her that it is not mission impossible!

Be creative in making your kit. Draw an open briefcase and then place items in it that help to control anger (see figure 6.8). It may be that you have discussed the strategies but that this will help to pull it all together.

Here are some examples of what could go in the kit:

- A disguise such as for a 'laidback cool dude'. This helps the child to remember that relaxation is important.
- A pair of special neutralizing anger glasses that, when put on, allows the wearer to see the world in a less angry way. Explain to the child that when you are angry you tend to view the world in a negative way, which makes it more likely that you will respond to people in an aggressive manner. It

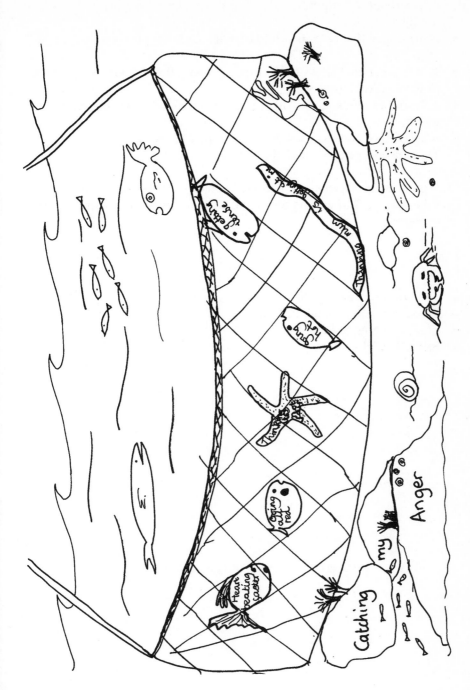

Figure 6.7   Catching My Anger

is important to learn how to replace these angry thoughts with positive thoughts.

- A magic pen that helps the child to write out his or her thoughts and feelings.
- A stopwatch that slows down time, allowing the wearer to count to ten slowly and calm down.
- A cushion with 'anger' written on it, to punch when feeling really frustrated.
- A list of the people who are helping the child to overcome his or her anger. These people can be called 'the back-up team'.

Once the strategies have been discussed you can ask the child to make a note over the next week of which parts of the kit he or she used to help control his or her temper.

SEE ALSO

- The Winning Team (p. 87)
- The Conquering Soldier (CT1, p. 87)
- Clear Thinking (CT1, p. 84)
- Self-talk (CT1, p. 93)

The Anger De-bugging Kit

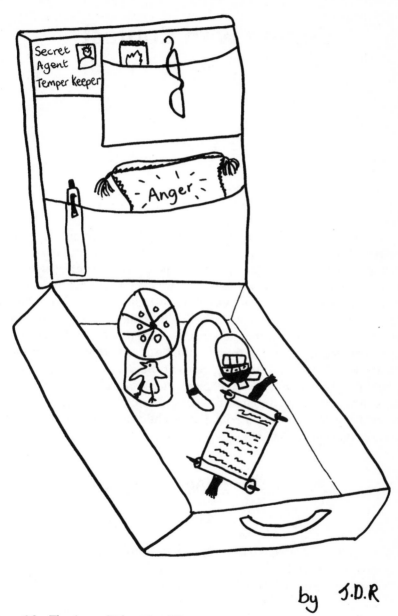

Figure 6.8   The Anger Debugging Kit

Chapter 7

Coping with Contact

As with any situation where two separate families are involved, the child may experience problems over contact. Very often this can lead to disturbed behaviour both before and after contact has taken place. If contact is frequent, the carers may feel as if their whole lives are overshadowed by it. For the child, it often feels like he or she is torn between the adults in his or her life. Sometimes the adults do not help, by telling the child not to tell other adults about what happens when they are together. Even without this additional pressure, resolution will not be found until the child is able to accept that he or she can love both or all sets of parents at the same time. The following activities are designed to help that happen. Please be careful in their use and adapt as necessary to suit the circumstances of the child. It is very easy, when approaching such sensitive material, for the child to feel that you are siding with one or other set of parents.

Torn to Shreds (Age: 7–14 years)

AIM

To help the child who is feeling torn between those involved in their parenting and to show the child that you understand these feelings. To provide strategies to help reduce these feelings of being torn.

Materials

A4 paper, pens and pencils, eraser and blank sticky label.

Method

First, ask the child to draw a picture of him or herself in the centre of the page (older children can write their names). Then write the names of all the adults who have some sort of parenting claim in the child's life around the name or picture.

Discuss with the child that sometimes children in their position can feel very confused about all the adults who are caring for them. They can sometimes feel as if the adults want different things and they do not know what to do. As you discuss this, listen to how the child describes it. In our experience children often come up with phrases of their own to describe their feelings, such as 'torn in half', 'they pull me this way and that' or 'I feel torn to shreds'.

If the child denies these feelings, but you are fairly sure from the behaviour that he or she is feeling torn, then re-start the activity as if it is another child. Use your knowledge of the child to influence the ideas and strategies and involve the child by using phrases like 'What do you think we should tell Tommy he should do?'. Sometimes, as you proceed through the activity, the child begins to say that Tommy is 'like me', or 'that's what I'd do, when my Mum says that'. Sometimes the child knows very well that the work is about him or herself, but he or she is happy to continue anyway.

Write a title on the piece of work that reflects the child's feelings using his or her terminology, e.g. 'Torn to Shreds'or 'All Muddled Up'. Link the adults to the child using pencil. Discuss with the child how the pencil lines are like ropes, pulling the child in different directions. You may want to spend some time talking about this.

Tell the child that together you could think of some strategies to help reduce these feelings of being 'torn', which you can discuss with the adults. Write these on the picture, beside the person it relates to. Encourage the child to write the statements beside the adults and not beside the picture of the child.

Here are some examples from our work:

- My social worker can talk to Mummy and ask her not to keep checking that I love her.
- I can tell my Mummy that I don't like to go to Brownies late when I have to wait for her to phone. I can ask my social worker to help me with this.
- I can try and talk to my foster Mum about how I feel, and tell her I don't know who to love.

- My foster Mum might let me take some of my toys so that I can show them to Mummy at the contact place.

Once you have come up with some useful strategies and written them on the original drawing, rub out the pencil lines. You could then put a sticky label over the title 'Torn to Shreds' and rename the activity with a positive title, e.g. 'Surrounded by Love' or 'Everyone Cares'.

Sharing and Caring (Age: 6 years and upwards)

AIM

To help the child understand the roles of various adults in his or her life.

MATERIALS

Several sheets of A4 paper, colouring pens or fine drawing pen.

METHOD

This activity may take more than one session.

As preparation for the activity, discuss with the children the ways in which different people feature in their lives. For example, it may be that the children look like their birth parents to a certain extent, they enjoy seeing them, they buy them things and they love them. The present carer provides their everyday needs, comforts them, looks after them, provides their pocket money and loves them.

The information gathered then can be recorded in the form of a cartoon with the child drawing him or herself asking the question "What do you do?" of each of the characters and ending with a picture of the child saying 'And what do I do? Well, maybe I just feel safe!' or some other phrase that positively reflects the fact that there are many people who care for him or her. If the child says that he or she feels confused, then this is quite acceptable to put on the cartoon. However, remind the child that you will work together to help him or her to feel less confused.

A younger child may prefer to draw a separate page for each person, with the final page reflecting some of the things that he or she does, e.g. 'I pick up my toys' as well as feelings such as 'I feel happy living with Barbara'.

Adolescents may prefer to do this activity without the cartoon, phrasing the questions in the third person, e.g. 'What do they do?', and writing the answers underneath.

SEE ALSO

l The People Puzzle (p. 36)
l Portions of Parenting (CT1, p. 115)

Love Grows (Age: 8–12 years)

AIM

To help children understand that they can love more than one set of parents at the same time.

MATERIALS

A4 paper, colouring pens, balloons.

METHOD

Blow up a balloon and show it to the child. Talk about the balloon being full of air and how that is like him or her being full of love for Mum (or whichever parenting adult seems to be most consistently loved). Then pick up another balloon and blow it up. We suggest that you do not say anything about this balloon until you are sure it will inflate easily. As you begin to fill it with air, explain that even though you have filled one, there is enough air to fill another, and another (as you blow it up), and another.

Talk to the child about how love keeps on coming, if you let it, and just as there is enough air to fill balloons, so the child has enough love to love all those important people in his or her life at once. Explain that it is still good to love the absent parent or parents, but that love need not get in the way of loving those who look after him or her now.

Depending on the circumstances, you may be able to help the child feel that he or she has permission from the adults around to love both carers and parents at the same time. If the carers are agreeable, they may be willing to reinforce this message both in the session and at home.

Complete the activity by writing down what the child has learnt from the balloons. Help the child to draw balloons on this piece of work, if they want to. The sentences about the work can be written in the balloons (see figure 7.1).

It is suggested that the balloons do not go home with the child, because by

Love Grows

I have enough
love to go
around

I can still
love my mother

It is ok
to love my
new family

Figure 7.1 Love Grows

nature they will gradually deflate – maybe giving an unwanted message to the child!

Variation: Overflowing Love

If you have access to a sink with running water and two glasses, the same message can be given by demonstrating that more than one glass can be filled to overflowing with water. Talk about how we can feel love 'overflowing' to others and ask the child about how he or she feels. Finish the activity by draw-

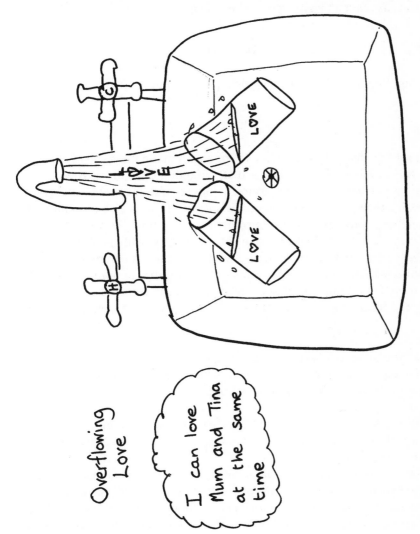

Figure 7.2 Overflowing Love

ing the picture of the running tap and full glasses, with the water splashing into both and the caption 'I can love . . . and . . . at the same time' (see figure 7.2).

Managing Many (Age: 11 years and upwards)

AIM

To help children realize that they can manage many areas of their life very well, and that contact visits also can be managed.

MATERIALS

Three juggling balls (if you can juggle!), pen and paper.

METHOD

Introduce the idea of how we have to cope with many things all at once. Describe this as being like juggling, actually juggling the balls as you do so, if you can. Involve the children in trying to juggle – if they cannot cope with all three balls, then see how they get on with two. If this is also difficult to do, then set them multi-tasking in some other way. For example, ask them to hop while they clap. Try to make this part of the activity really good fun, so that they feel pleased that they are coping with more than one thing at a time.

Discuss with the child how we manage lots of things in our lives, all at the same time. Do a brainstorming exercise, writing it down as you go, using mostly the child's suggestions. The kind of things you are looking for would be:

- Walking along while chatting to a friend
- Dancing and listening to music while thinking about something else
- Being a friend while being a school pupil

Help the child to consider bigger areas, e.g. managing money while being friends with more than one person at a time and doing lots of different subjects at school.

Go on to a second sheet of paper to brainstorm about relationships that are managed all at the same time. This page may have the child's name or 'Me' in the middle of the page and everyone else's names around it. Use this to talk about any difficulties the child may have in managing any of the relationships, and how he or she feels about them. The child may wish to draw dotted lines to people where the relationship is not too good, with unbroken ones where the relationship is 'all right' and double lines for really strong, good relationships (see figure 7.3).

Finish the session with the firm message that the child is able to manage relating to lots of people at the same time, with a sentence to confirm this written on the bottom of the piece of work. The child may like to sign by this sentence as a signal of his or her willingness to try to manage many relationships well.

S<small>EE</small> <small>ALSO</small>

- The People Puzzle (p. 36)

Managing Many

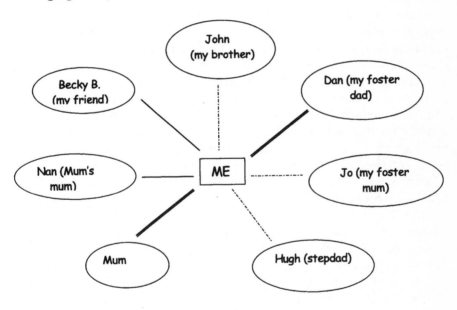

I can manage lots of things at the same time. Even all my relationships! I know it is okay to love Mum and Jo at the same time.

Figure 7.3 Managing Many

No Need for Stealthy Secrets
(Age: 7 years and upwards)

Aim

To teach the child that some secrets should not be kept and to resist adult pressure, even from birth parents or carers, to keep secrets.

Materials

Two sheets of A3 or A4 paper, colouring pens, scissors and glue stick.

Method

Allow plenty of time for this activity in case difficult secrets are divulged.

Brainstorm with the child all the secrets that he or she has ever been asked to keep. Explain that these can be old secrets as well as current ones. Lead into discussion by giving prompts in the form of questions, e.g. 'Are there times when you thought you'd be in trouble when you kept a secret?' 'Are there adults who have asked you to keep secrets?' 'Are some secrets really good?' 'Are some secrets bad?' 'What about secrets to do with birthdays, or surprise holidays?' 'Do your friends ask you to keep secrets?'.

As the child talks, be writing down, or encourage the child to write down, the collection of secrets. Keep the writing fairly small, because several sentences will need to fit in a quarter of your paper.

When you have a page full of secrets, take the second piece of paper. Head it 'No need for Stealthy Secrets' or similar, to suit the child's developmental level. Divide the rest of the page in four, with headings 'Secrets I love to keep', 'Secrets that worry me', 'Secrets I should never have to keep' and 'Secrets that keep me safe'. The child may wish to put some illustrations in the boxes. Help the child sort out the page of secrets that he or she has already written, cutting out the ones appropriate to him or her and sticking them in the right place on the poster (see figure 7.4).

An adolescent may wish to copy the secrets under the appropriate headings and not illustrate the piece of work.

Be prepared for the child possibly to disclose abuse or worrying secrets during this piece of work. If this happens, reassure the child that he or she has done exactly the right thing in telling you and what you will now be doing to keep him or her safe. Follow child protection guidelines and speak to your manager and/or the child's social worker, as appropriate.

Figure 7.4 No Need for Stealthy Secrets

As always with emotional work, make sure that by the end of the session the child feels safe. Involve the carer, if appropriate, in this. Reassure the child that you can continue to talk these things through at the next session if he or she wants to, so that the child feels that he or she is leaving these difficult secrets with you and not taking them back home.

SEE ALSO

- What Happens Next? (p. 38)
- The People Puzzle (p. 36)
- Scared Sally and Brave Belinda (p. 70)
- Safety Hand (CT1, p.70)
- Safety Soldier (CT1, p.87)

Chapter 8

Solving Problems

The activities in this chapter will help a child to develop new skills in resolving behavioural problems or in making decisions. Some of the child's difficulties may have arisen in past places where he or she has lived because of the child's needs. For example, disruptive behaviour may have had the function of gaining much-needed attention. Even though attention is freely available in the new environment, the learnt behaviour lingers on. Learning how to overcome these difficulties and to problem-solve will help the child in other ways, such as promoting self-efficacy.

The Winning Team (Age: 7 –13 years)

AIM

To help children overcome a problem by helping them to realize that there are people and strategies to help them. To help motivate them to change.

MATERIALS

A4 paper, colouring pens or pencils, stickers.

Method

To prepare, discuss with the children anyone or anything that helps them with their problem and make a list of these. You may already know some of them from previous sessions. Then discuss anything that gets in the way of them being able to overcome their problem, e.g. forgetfulness. Liken this to a game of football (or any other similar team game) where on their team are all the players that represent the things that are going to help them. On the other team are the players that represent the things that stop them from overcoming their difficulty. Each time they use a strategy or accept help, they are scoring a goal and demoralizing the opposing team. Use team game talk such as 'beating the team' and 'winning the game' to help the child feel really motivated to change.

Next draw a pitch on the page with goalposts at each end. Let the child draw his or her players on one half of the pitch with labels for the person or strategy they represent. For the more keen footballers, the players could be placed in relevant positions. On the other side of the pitch (maybe around the goal post) draw the other team. You could get the child to think of a good name for his or her team, such as the 'All Stars', and he or she could even come up with a name for the other side, such as 'The Spoilers'.

This visual representation may be enough to help motivate a child who has lost his or her enthusiasm for overcoming a problem. However it can be taken a stage further with the pitch being used like a reward chart. So each time the child uses a strategy or accepts help, he or she gets a goal. Supply the child with some stickers with footballs drawn onto them and these can be placed in the winning goal post.

As with other reward-based systems, do not give any stickers for the chart for the child failing to earn the goals.

Our example in figure 8.1 is based on the work of a 7-year old.

See also

- I Can Do It Now (p. 95)
- The Battle (CT1, p.81)
- The Conquering Soldier (CT1, p.87)

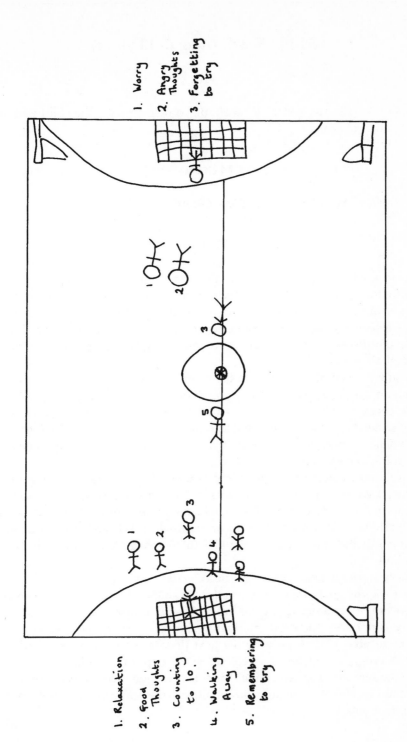

Figure 8.1 The Winning Team

Within Reach (Age: 6–13 years)

Aim

To set up a reward system for a child. To help provide the child with the motivation to change.

Materials

A4 paper, pens and an A4 thin piece of card.

Method

This reward chart can be used for all types of behavioural problems, from soiling to aggression. As with other reward systems, the child needs to be very clear what he or she needs to do in order to get a reward. The goals have to be achievable. Rewards should never be taken away and a reward chart should be used only for the purpose of rewarding, not recording the problem behaviour.

You will need discussion with the carers before this activity, to decide on small appropriate rewards. Once you know what the carer is happy to provide, check with the child that these rewards will be worked for. The rewards always need to be something that the child wants or will consider special.

Explain to children that in order to help them overcome their problem you are going to make a reward chart with them.

Draw a wall on the A4 paper and explain to the child that you are going to draw (or write) some prizes or tokens on the wall for the child to collect with a ladder. At the top of the ladder will be the prize or reward that can be collected if the child has achieved his or her final goal. Together you can work on the wall and, if desired, you could actually make a ladder to reach the top from A4 card.

Each step on the ladder needs to be a clearly defined goal. As can be seen in figure 8.2, the goals are in very small steps so that they are easily attainable. There are prizes as specific goals are reached but these are not necessary for every step. If the child needs motivating, however, it may be good for him or her to receive a token towards the next prize as each step is reached. The child's progress is recorded by colouring the steps of the ladder.

Make sure the progress up the ladder is reviewed each time you meet with the child and involve the carers in keeping up the praise the child will need to keep motivated.

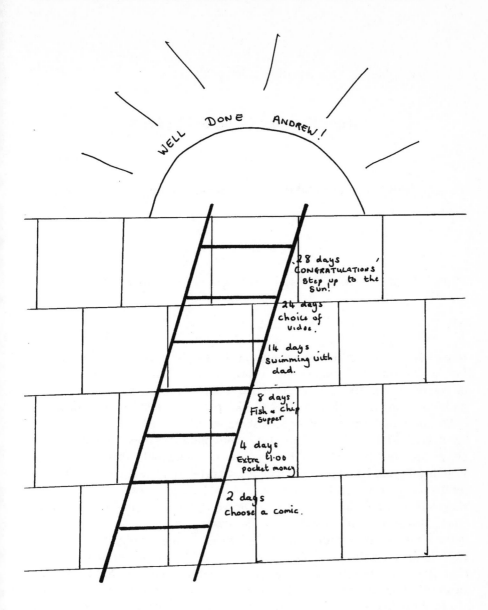

Figure 8.2   Within Reach

- Zoro Reaches the Mountain Top (CT1, p.38)

Target Practice (Age: 6–13 years)

AIM

To help a child to understand that it can take effort and practice to change a behaviour.

MATERIALS

Three balls or three rolled up socks, wastepaper bin, pens and A4 paper.

METHOD

Make sure that the room you are using is fairly large and that there are no breakables around! To begin with, do a warm up and throw a ball to the child; as you do so, talk about the skill needed to throw and catch. Try exchanging balls, throwing them to each other and keep the pace fast and light-hearted.

For the actual activity, place a wastepaper bin or bucket about 2 m away from the child. Have a competition with the child to see how many balls he or she can get into the bucket. If this is too easy, move a bit further away until it is quite difficult. The child should be able to get the ball in sometimes, but not all the time. Start counting how many of the balls go in each time he or she throws 3. You are looking for a point at which there is some improvement. This is easier to see if you are writing it down.

Once there is some improvement (or if there is none but the child is becoming bored), talk to the child about the way he or she has practised and within that short space of time has already made an improvement. Discuss how he or she did this – perhaps by talking about the strategies used, such as aiming a little more to the left or throwing in more of an arc. Point out that the child could work out what was going wrong and then try to correct it. This is where you bring up the similarities between learning to throw a ball in a bin more accurately and learning to overcome a habit or improve a skill such as controlling a temper. Discuss how the child may have tried before but used the wrong strategies. Writing down your findings will help the child make the most of the analogy. An example is presented below.

Target practice

Today we have used juggling balls and improved our aim. We have found out that:

- Practice makes perfect
- We have to keep going
- We have to change the way we do it if our strategies do not work

This is like controlling my temper:

- I must practice noticing when I am getting mad
- I must keep trying to control it
- If one thing does not work I will try something else

Variation 1: Flying Targets

If you have a large space, the same activity can be carried out with paper planes (see Appendix 2). In this case you may be trying to improve on distance of flight, rather than accuracy. Analogies can be made with keeping improved behaviours going for longer. The child can be encouraged to adapt the plane to fly better, for longer, while likening this to trying slightly different ways of improving behaviour, to see if that helps.

Try to make the session fun, and keep repeating the message you are trying to impart. It is useful to write up the session in the manner indicated above.

Variation 2: Juggling Genius (Age: 8 years and upwards)

If you have a child who is good at throwing the balls and if you can juggle, try to teach this to the child. Many children who cannot juggle with three balls can juggle with two. A different skill is needed for two balls because each ball is passed between the hands one at a time before being thrown in a circular movement. If three balls are used, each ball is thrown in the air in a rhythmic manner, but balls are never just passed between hands. When someone who can do two balls learns to juggle with three balls, a lot of passing takes place before he or she remembers always to throw.

This is a powerful visual aid for increasing motivation. The exercise can help to teach children that we tend to revert to bad habits or ways of behaving even while we are trying to learn new ways. This can then be related to their behaviour, to help them overcome times when they slip back.

SEE ALSO

- Practice Makes Perfect (CT1, p.68)

Test and Try (Age: 10 years and upwards)

AIM

To help the child 'experiment' with more acceptable behaviours.

MATERIALS

Pens, paper (preferably lined file paper), ruler.

METHOD

This activity requires follow-up in subsequent sessions.

Although this is a useful exercise to help the child overcome many behavioural difficulties, it seems to be most effective for children who are trying to control their anger. It is not recommended for a child who hates science, unless he or she is keen to undertake this 'experiment'.

Help children to 'analyse' a difficult episode where they, for example, lost their temper and ended up getting into trouble. Talk with them about ways of diffusing (or maybe defusing?) or getting out of the situation, so that there is not a negative outcome.

With the child, create some specific strategies that may prove effective. Then talk about the best way to carry this out, recording the results.

Make out (or have ready prepared) a format for writing up the 'experiment' of behaving in a different way. Children may decide that they do not want to tell their carers about the experiment, but would rather see if the carers notice anything for themselves.

A good format for writing up the experiment could be:

- What are we testing?
- How are we testing it?
- What have we found out?

An older child may prefer to have:

- Hypothesis
- Method
- Results
- Discussion

Alternatively, they may wish to match the style they use in their science lessons. Help children write up the first two sections in your session. Make it look fairly neat and business-like. Ask them to make notes ready for writing up the rest, or if they are very confident with their writing they can do it themselves, ready for when you review the experiment.

Encourage the child to run the experiment until your next session, or for at least two weeks, recording the results for discussion. When discussing it, try to emphasize any minor successes and talk about ways of building on those. If the experiment has failed completely, talk about why, and whether the new strategies were too difficult. Write the rest of the experiment up.

The child may well be willing to redesign the experiment in the light of the results, and try again!

See also

- Grumbling Gertie and Merry Maud (p. 67)
- The Anger Debugging Kit (p. 72)
- I Can Help (CT1, p. 66)
- Practice Makes Perfect (CT1, p. 68)

I Can Do It (Now) (Age: 6–12 years)

Aim

To review progress made and to help think about new goals for the future.

Materials

A4 paper and colouring pens.

Method

This is a good activity to use near a child's birthday.

Explain to the child that he or she is going to think about how much progress has been made and what has been achieved over the last year. Together you are going to make a poster to show this information. Write 'I can do it !' at the top of page and then ask the child to write his or her name in the middle of the page. Together, brainstorm some of the important things that the child would like to write down about what he or she has done. Give some prompts, if necessary, including several aspects of the child's life, e.g. home, school, therapy, friends and hobbies. Place all the positive statements around the child's name.

On another page think about some goals for the future. This page could be labelled 'Now I am . . . I am going to', with the child's age at the birthday filled in. Then the new, realistic goals for the coming year can be placed around the page.

Together with the child, think about some first steps towards achieving these goals, keeping each step easily achievable.

Variation: I Am Here Now

This is very similar to the above activity, but even more relevant when helping a child adjust to a new home and family. The activity involves asking the child to contrast where he or she used to live and behave, with how he or she behaves and/or feels now. Label the page 'I am here now' and encourage the child to write down some of the ways things have changed. Inventive children may enjoy putting this information in a spidergraph (see figure 8.3). Make it very positive and celebrate the progress they have made. Then ask the child to think about what he or she would like to change now, including what present difficulties he or she would like to overcome. Again, these can be written on a separate page.

You may need to spend time talking about any losses which the child may mention during this activity. Try to end on a positive, forward-looking note. See also:

- Just Me (p. 44)
- I'll Get There Someday (p. 107)
- The Flowing River (p. 103)
- Crazy Dreams and Winning Wishes (p. 106)
- Best Achievements (CT1, p. 127)
- Past, Present, Future (CT1, p. 129)
- The Story So Far (CT1, p. 132)

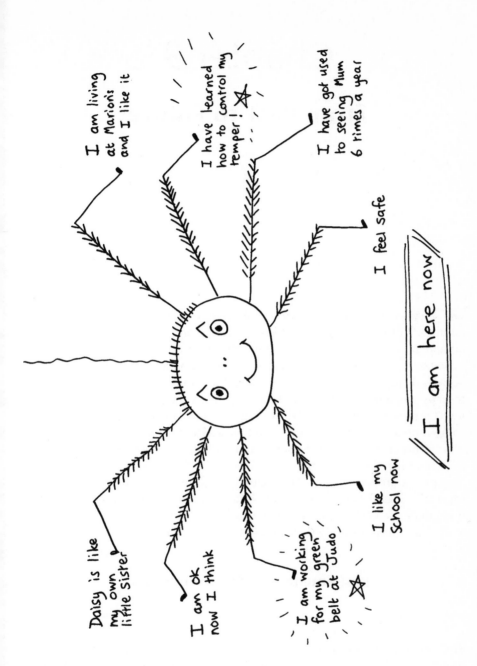

Figure 8.3 I Am Here Now

Chapter 9

From Past to Future

Life story work has proved very useful in helping children who have moved families. Authors like Ryan and Walker (1993) and Fahlberg (1994) have all documented ways of working to help the child understand what has happened to him or her in the past and why. The activities here will supplement or extend some of their ideas, translating them into tasks that can be used in therapy when tailored to the child's needs. However, whatever the plans for the children, they need to be encouraged to find areas where they do have some control of their lives, and learn that decisions made now can influence their future. This work need not be left until last, in fact it is often very useful to do it at any time when the child is 'stuck' and unable to benefit from the care that is around to help. The following activities have been found to be especially useful for this group of children, even in some cases where the immediate plan is to move to a new family, because they help give the child control and responsibility that can assist in promoting a sense of stability.

Past Patchwork (Age: 6–14 years)

Aim

To help children see that the memories they have, however few they are, mount up and are important. To provide a 'summary' of the memories the child has.

Materials

A3 paper (or A4 if the activity is to go in a Life Story Book), colouring pens, fine pen for writing, piece of patchwork (optional).

Method

Explain to the child that we all have memories of incidents or feelings that have happened to us in the past. Some of these are good memories whereas others are not so pleasant. Some of these memories are just snippets like little scraps of material that are put together to make a patchwork quilt. If you have a piece of material patchwork, bringing it to the session will add a useful visual aid.

Help the child draw a patchwork quilt, complete with stitching. The patches will need to be large enough to take at least one sentence of writing. In the squares of the quilt, at random intervals, write the memories the child has – scatter these around, not worrying too much about chronological order. Try to encourage the child to think of many positive memories, but include the difficult ones as well.

Let the child colour in the patches as you go, decorating them if desired. While the colouring is being done, it is usually a very good time to encourage children to talk about any difficult memories and help them to come to terms with the fact that some things they remember are not good. When you write them on the quilt, try to phrase them so that the child is not traumatized each time the piece of work is reviewed, and in wording that will not cause the child embarrassment if it is seen by a friend.

When you have run out of memories to write in, you and/or the child can colour in the remaining squares with plain, fairly pastel colours (see figure 9.1). Explain to the child that these blank squares can be ready to note anything else that pops into his or her memory. As you finish the session, spend time talking about the best memory, so that the child leaves the session feeling good.

This activity can form the basis of a memory book, with each memory being expanded upon, perhaps by a page of writing or drawings, as the book is made up.

Variation: Sticky Patches

Extra materials needed: Coloured paper and glue stick, or coloured gummed sheets, scissors.

A similar idea can be made into an activity that uses a cognitive approach

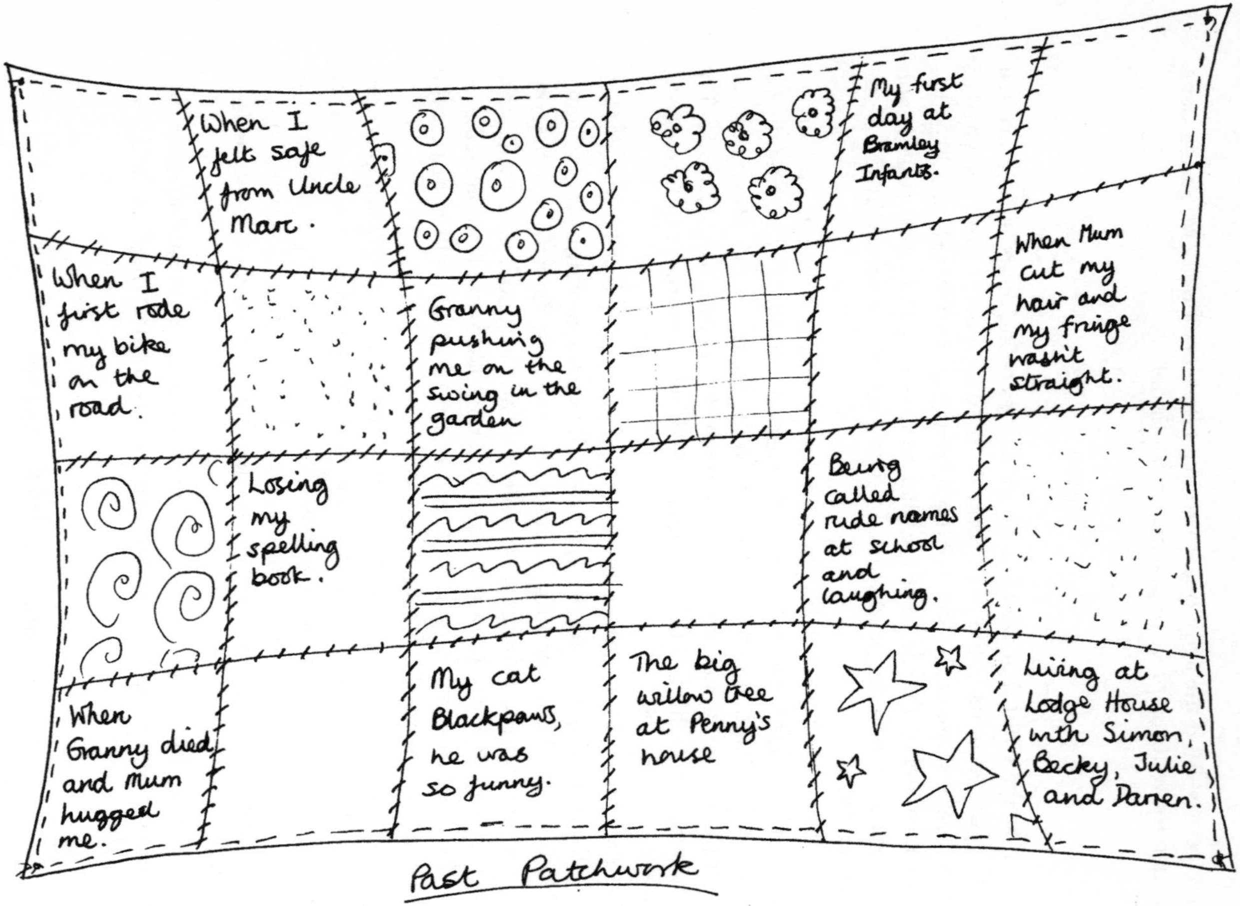

My first day at Bramley Infants.

When Mum cut my hair and my fringe wasn't straight.

When I felt safe from Uncle Marc.

Granny pushing me on the swing in the garden.

Being called rude names at school and laughing.

Living at Lodge House with Simon, Becky, Julie and Darren.

When I first rode my bike on the road.

Losing my spelling book.

My cat Blackpaws, he was so funny.

The big willow tree at Penny's house.

When Granny died and Mum hugged me.

Past Patchwork

Figure 9.1 Past Patchwork

for past hurts. This is done by encouraging the child to write any unpleasant memories (sticky patches) on coloured paper or gummed paper. These are then cut out to fit somewhere within an outline of a quilt. The unpleasant memories are discussed, and where appropriate the outcome of the discussion is stuck over the patch. For example, if the child has written 'Because I was naughty I had to go away', it may be that after discussion the child is able to understand that there are many reasons why adults cannot cope, and that children are sometimes naughty because they are unhappy. They can then appreciate that it is not the child's fault. A fresh patch may read something like 'The grown-ups all decided I would be better living with Susan' (Susan being the foster mother).

Sometimes using this activity can encourage the child to remember that good things have happened since the bad times. The child then can be encouraged to stick the good memory over the bad. An example would be if the child can remember being frightened by a dog, but then has a more recent memory of a very special dog that he or she loved very much. The second memory patch can be stuck over the first.

Some unpleasant memories will not be able to be covered over. This may indicate that there are areas that the child needs help on in future sessions. Discuss these memories with the child, recognizing that he or she feels angry or unhappy about them. Do not finish the session before filling in some of the blank patches with more good memories or going back to some of the positive memories you have already found. Any 'stitches' will need to be drawn on afterwards. While this is being done, encourage the child to focus on a good memory as you finish the activity. If none are forthcoming, be careful to finish the session with some positives from their present lives, or things they are looking forward to.

SEE ALSO

- The Story So Far (CT1, p.132)

My Story (Age: 6 years and upwards)

AIM

To write a book with children about themselves, including their feelings. This can be used as part of life story work.

MATERIALS

Colouring pens, scissors, glue stick, project folder and A4 paper. Access to a computer (optional).

METHOD

This activity takes the form of a book written in the third person, which can be particularly useful for a child who does not want to work directly with his or her experiences. The activity is likely to take several sessions and can be typed up on a computer between sessions, with any illustrations being cut out and glued into the appropriate places. If possible, let the child choose how you will be doing it.

You will need to explain to the child that you are going to write a book together about him or herself. Agree on a title that puts them in the third person, e.g. 'The tales of Jenny's travels'.

Before writing anything down, ask the child what would be really important to put in the book. If the child is not forthcoming, then draw on your knowledge of the child to make a few suggestions. Try to obtain the permission of the child before anything goes in the book. Obviously, the content will then vary according to the child, but could include taking the child through some of the main life events, such as house moves, schools attended, moves to different families, holidays, etc.

The book needs to be written in clear, age-appropriate language. Encourage the child to take full part in the preparation of the book, perhaps by writing it in his or her own words, or by preparing drawings to be pasted against the text. Even if you are handwriting the book, it is a good idea for the child to do the drawings separately because this will mean that you can both be working on the same topic at the same time. Do not do too many pages at once, because this can be very exhausting work for the child.

Somewhere on each page write 'How did (insert name of child) feel then' and leave a gap for the child to fill in the emotion. If the child cannot cope with this, be ready with a list of emotions from which he or she can choose. To help the younger child, draw pictures of little faces demonstrating different emotions for the child to circle. Be prepared to set aside the work while you discuss a particularly difficult or traumatic event. It is important that the child finishes this activity on a positive note each session, so when reviewing the work, end on one of the positive attributes or events for that child.

Variation: A Cartoon about Life (Age: 11 years and upwards)

This is similar to 'My Story' and is suitable for those children who have shown some artistic flair. The child and therapist can come up with a cartoon character to represent the child. This character then goes through the child's life marking important moves and events. It is easier if there is some script under each cartoon illustration, but use speech bubbles as appropriate. Let the child draw the cartoons and fill in the emotions as before.

If the child cannot do this directly about him or herself, you may need to do it as an analogy. For example:

'Whoosh! Sonic the Hedgehog suddenly found himself in a very strange place. He wondered if there were special rules about being in this place. Should he go downstairs in the morning, or stay up here in his sleeping quarters? He did not know what to do. He felt very . . . '

The illustration drawn above the example text could have Sonic saying 'Where am I?' or 'I am frightened. I don't know where I am'.

See also

- Past, Present, Future (CT1, p.129)
- My Life So Far (CT1, p.133)

The Flowing River (Age: 7 years and upwards)

Aim

To review children's lives, exploring both the bad and good experiences and showing how these make children who they are. To think about future goals.

Materials

A4 paper, colouring pens, pencil and eraser.

Method

Explain to the child that the past, present and future is going to be drawn as a flowing river. Encourage the child to draw in pencil a river winding across the page and ending up flowing into a pool or lake. The child can then fill the flowing river in with short descriptions of how things were. The right chronological order is not too important for this exercise. The child could draw rocks to represent difficult or bad experiences, waterfalls to represent exciting times, calm waters to represent stable times. The river could eventually flow into an open pool where future wishes are written about.

At this stage the child may wish to go over the initial pencil drawing to produce a final piece of work.

Once completed, review the piece of work with the child. Depending on the age of the child, there is plenty of scope to draw comparisons between the river and the child. For example, you could highlight that the river has hidden depths, things that are not seen, just like the child who may also be hiding feelings from others. You can also highlight that the river is important to so many things, that it sustains life. In the same way, the child is extremely important to other people.

Variation: Flowing On

The same idea can be used to focus on the losses in the child's life. Draw a river and use this to discuss how the river flows along, but some of the branches and leaves floating in it get caught on the banks and left behind (see figure 9.2). The banks themselves, and any rocks or islands, stay where they are while the river flows on. Talk to the child about how people and places in his or her life have been left behind. However, the child's own life goes on and he or she moves to fresh places, experiences and relationships. Allow the child time to talk about feelings of loss and recognize these with him or her.

Have a box of tissues handy, to pass quietly to the child if he or she starts to cry. Write some of the losses on the bank of the river. Talk about how the memories of these things will go with the child, and write 'memories' in the water.

As you continue to draw the picture together, try to give children a sense of hope by talking about anything that they find good about their life now. Make your river run into a pool and write these things around its banks. Label the pool 'now' or 'my present life'. Spend time talking about this and about who supports the child and cares for the child now, or something the child really enjoys where he or she lives now. For the child who needs to feel secure in the present, this may be the point at which the activity ends. For others, it may be important to draw the river running from the pool into the future. In another session follow this up with some work on the future, perhaps using one of the following two activities.

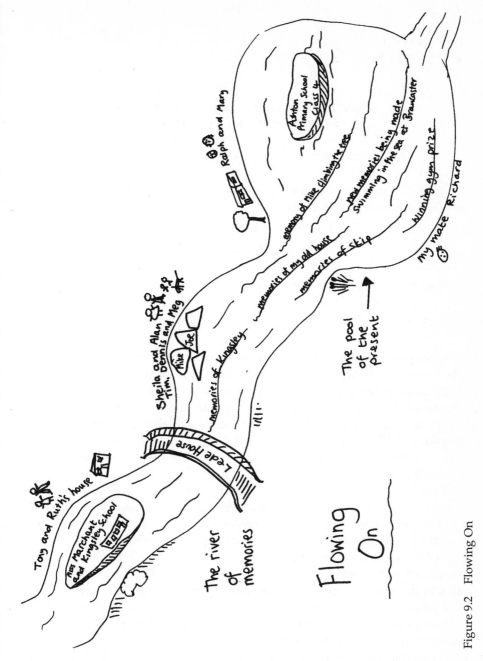

Figure 9.2 Flowing On

Crazy Dreams and Winning Wishes
(Age: 6 years and upwards)

AIM

To help the child sort out realistic wishes and fantasy. To give the message that some wishes are achievable.

MATERIALS

Two sheets of A4 paper, colouring pens.

METHOD

This is a pen and paper activity. Discuss with the children what they want for the future. Encourage them by talking about how other people (or yourself) want to do things, and how some of those things really come about and others do not. Talk about if they had a lot of money, how could they use it? Or if they could go anywhere in the world, where would they go? If they could do anything at all, what would they do? If they could choose any career in the future, what would it be? Who would they be in contact with and where would they live?

Take notes ready for the picture as the child fantasizes. Then lead the child into thinking more realistically about what he or she wants. You may well find that initial thoughts are still fantasies, so guide the child. If you are talking about careers, ask what sort of things the child likes and is good at, in or out of school, and suggest an appropriate type of career. For example, 'with maths' or 'with animals' could be a possibility. If the child is not sure, reflect that in the wish, e.g. 'A job with animals, or using computers or maths'. Do not be afraid to talk about relationships with this piece of work, e.g. let the child talk about wanting to meet birth father or birth siblings and include the desires expressed as you would with any other subject.

Help the child put the title of the work right across the width of the paper, or use sub-titles (see figure 9.3). As the child transfers the ideas onto the picture, help him or her to sort them out into unlikely (crazy) and likely (winning) ones. If you are working with a very impulsive child, it may be preferable to use a separate sheet of paper and make this into a cut and paste exercise to minimize the possibility of all the 'crazy' dreams becoming 'winning', or 'possible', dreams.

For the ones where it is uncertain which category the wish should go in, place them near the middle. Similarly, if a child is adamant that something is not a crazy dream, encourage him or her to put it near the middle. Sometimes children are thinking negatively and something quite possible, like 'Have a dog of my own', is seen by them as crazy. Help them to take a long-term view and see that they will be able to make their own decisions about things like that when they are adults.

Just occasionally you may need to find out information before you can guide the child as to whether a dream is realistic or impossible. This is less likely if you are fully up-to-date with the plans for the child. Discuss any difficult ones with the child and agree to leave the item off until you have found out about them, preferably by the next session.

End the activity by talking about the Winning Wishes and the way these can be achieved.

This is a good activity to use before breaking down the way to achieve a dream into very small goals. For example, if the child wants to be a motor mechanic, he or she will need to do all the technology coursework and apply for a college course. The very small goal may be to do three pages of the overdue coursework by the weekend. 'First Steps Forward' in CT1 describes this in greater detail.

Variation: Dreamboxes

A similar activity can be done by writing lots of dreams or wishes onto small cards. For this activity you will need three boxes with slits in the lids (see Appendix 1). Label them Crazy Dreams, Winning Wishes, and 'Wannabes' (or a similar phrase to suggest that they are almost out of reach). Let the child or yourself write the wishes onto the cards and then discuss them before they are posted into the appropriate box. When the boxes are opened, list the information on a sheet under the headings and discuss first steps to achieving the Winning Wishes, as above.

See also

- Stairway To My Future (CT1, p. 97)
- First Steps Forward (CT1, p. 97)

Figure 9.3   Crazy Dreams and Winning Wishes

I'll Get There Someday (Age: 7 years and upwards)

AIM

To help children to think about how things have changed for them and how they may be in the future. To help them think about where they would like to be in the future and what their goals are.

MATERIALS

A4 or A3 paper, pens and pencils.

Method

Draw a series of overlapping bubbles, as in figure 9.4, with smaller bubbles at the top and larger bubbles at the bottom. Each bubble will represent a 3-year time period (if the child is under 10 years old you may want to make this a smaller span of years). Write the ages the child was, or will be, in each of the bubbles. Usually this can be taken up to around the time when the child is likely to be a parent themselves, perhaps mid-twenties or early thirties.

Ask children to think about what happened when they were younger and together write this in the 3-year blocks. Help them to consider the progress they have made. Then go on to consider what they think may happen in each of the coming 3-year blocks. When it comes to thinking about the future, help them to consider how old they will be and what they may be doing, e.g. 'living in my own flat'. Think about the problems they may have overcome at each point and the opportunities they would like to have.

Encourage them to talk about their feelings as you work through this. For example, discuss which parts they may find difficult and which parts they are looking forward to. Once the information is obtained for each 3-year block, the children may want to decorate their work. This can then be displayed or go in their folder, as appropriate.

As you complete this activity, draw together all the positive points from the work, leaving the child with a positive outlook for the future.

See also

- Past, Present, Future (CT1, p.129)

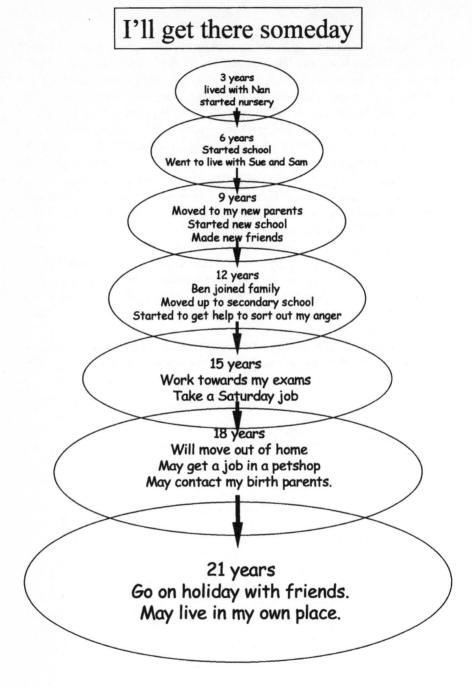

Figure 9.4   I'll Get There Someday

Appendix 1   Box Template Instructions

Enlarge the template until it only just fits on an A4 sheet. (The dimensions will be approximately 4.5 cm × 4.5 cm × 3 cm.) Lay the template on thin card to draw the outline. Cut round the outer edge. Score lightly across all other lines ready to be folded. Fold into the box shape along the scored lines. Fold the flaps in and glue them inside the box.

If you are using the box to post strips of card, cut a narrow slit in the top, as shown in figure A1.1.

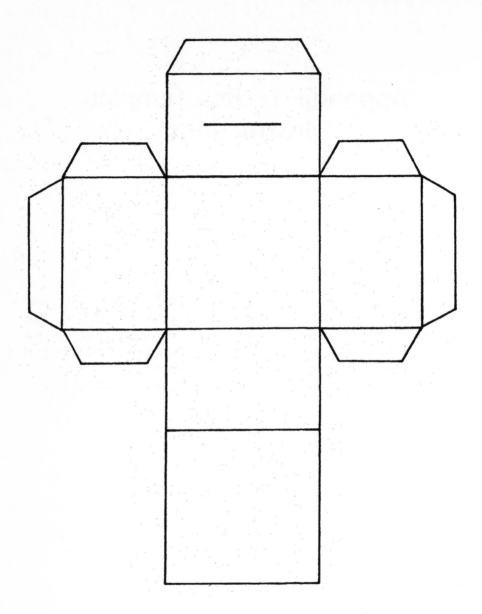

Figure A1.1   Box Template

Appendix 2   Paper Plane Instructions

Take a sheet of A4 paper and fold it down the middle lengthways. Fold the front corner of each side back to the middle fold. Then repeat this again, as indicated in figure A2.1. Finally fold the two short straight edges to the centre fold. The plane is now ready to fly, but for younger children could be improved by well-placed dabs of glue to hold it together.

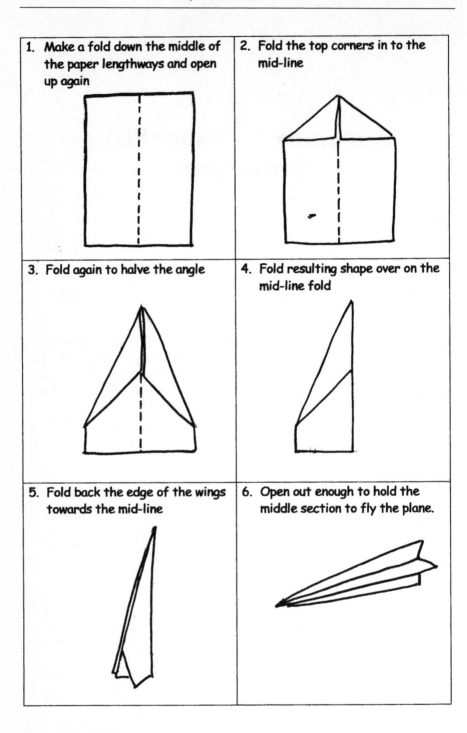

1. Make a fold down the middle of the paper lengthways and open up again

2. Fold the top corners in to the mid-line

3. Fold again to halve the angle

4. Fold resulting shape over on the mid-line fold

5. Fold back the edge of the wings towards the mid-line

6. Open out enough to hold the middle section to fly the plane.

Figure A2.1   Paper Plane

Appendix 3   Age and Child Development

The following guide to the relevant developmental stages may help you to judge whether the child you are working with can manage the task you present (for a more comprehensive description of developmental stages, see Fahlberg, 1994, Chapter 2). All children are different, so the guide only indicates roughly what children are usually like within the ages described.

Relevant information regarding emotional development is included to assist you in helping carers to understand their children's feelings and behaviour.

Birth–3 years

Children remain very dependent on their carers and have not fully developed language skills. Therapy with this age group is generally achieved through the training and educating of their carers, and therapy with such young children alone is relatively rare, except in cases of abuse/neglect or family problems where the child may provide information through disclosure. The activities in this book require interaction beyond the ability of this age group.

3–4 years

Most children of this age will have a vocabulary of between 1000 and 1500 words, so they will be beginning to understand and answer comprehensive questions. They increasingly use words, instead of temper tantrums, to show their independence. Their level of communication and understanding means that they can make simple bargains and can usually take turns. They enjoy simple games where they can use these skills. Be aware in therapy that children of this age seek to please, and thus may not appreciate the need to be honest.

Usually, 3–4-year-olds are able to comprehend simple emotions such as 'happy', 'sad' and 'angry', but may need to be given examples such as 'have a temper tantrum' for angry. They are starting to share and can play in a group with others. Although they may have some separation difficulties as they start nursery or playschool, they can usually settle and become confident in such surroundings. In the clinic setting, children of this age may want an older sibling or one of their parents in the room for added security.

4–5 years

Most 4–5-year-olds have extended their language to talk about the meanings of words. They can follow a two- or three- stage command, such as 'Pick up your toys, put them in the box and put on the lid'. They can understand opposites and use questions extensively. Control is an issue for many children because they now start seeking to please themselves, and this can lead to them being argumentative. Imagination is important at this age and children also enjoy humour in play, although they cannot necessarily understand or tell jokes successfully. They may still tell fanciful stories.

Once children have begun school their experiences broaden and for a while they may be struggling to cope with all the change. This can lead to some difficult behaviour, including being bossy and physically aggressive.

6–8 years

By the age of 6 years, children will be very active. It is a wriggly sort of age, with increased frustration and sometimes children regress to younger behaviour, including aggression and temper tantrums. Six-year-olds seem to swing from one end of the emotional scale to the other. They show enthusiasm at starting tasks but may have difficulty sticking with them without the encouragement of an adult. Because they still want physical closeness, many children may revert to needing a cuddly toy or sucking a thumb, even if this has been outgrown once. Taking things that belong to others is fairly normal and children commonly 'find' small items at school. They may call people names and tend to be verbally aggressive. In their general exploration of the world and how it works, they are sometimes cruel to animals. Response to praise is good, which means that reward systems are likely to be effective. Generally, children of this age will understand your therapy and be able to follow a programme.

Concentration generally improves by the age of 7 years and this means that children can be more involved in the preparation and running of therapy programmes. They may become engrossed in activities as they learn to concentrate better, giving adults the impression that they are being ignored. Children may still be forgetful and need to rely on adults. Being able to handle strong feelings is still difficult for 7-year-olds, who often end up fighting to resolve conflict or reduce tension. Children of this age cannot discuss how they feel while they are still upset, but may be able to later. They are usually poor at losing games and will sometimes cheat. However, they are beginning to develop a sense of fair play.

Seven-year-olds are able to understand another person's point of view (if this is explained to them), so can see how their own actions affect others. This is usually the youngest age for using activities that need this skill of seeing how others react, such as What Happens Next? (p. 38).

Eight-year-old children may appear more settled in many ways. They can be happy, cheeky and boastful, and may be conscientious in their work with you. Usually they can work well in groups, although they may criticize others but be upset if they lose face. Children who are 8 years old can usually begin to understand the process of time and its relevance to themselves. It is the earliest age at which activities involving the past and future may be relevant. As 8-year-olds are becoming more skilled at dealing with hurt they are less likely to respond with their fists. They are generally becoming more independent.

9–10 years

By 9 years of age children are beginning to plan ahead, which leads to hobbies such as collecting. They are less interested in fantasy games. They will respond to peer pressure and can work co-operatively in a group setting, although, because they prefer the company of their own gender, mixed groups can be hard work. A rising interest in activities such as sport may still be hampered by their wish to please their peers, rather than win. Nine-year-olds tend to respond to feelings of guilt and do not need to be told off to recognize right from wrong. They enjoy some responsibilities, which can be useful for therapy. They can, by now, process information to use it in different situations. This means that in therapy they will be able to recognize new circumstances where a freshly learnt behaviour will apply.

Friendships are of great importance to most 10-year-olds and may become of greater relevance to children than their own family. The gender difference widens because girls mature more quickly and look down on the boys. However, children of this age will still enjoy family outings, especially if they can take a friend. By this age, life begins to have meaning and they can enjoy working together with a therapist.

11–13 years

During adolescence the child will need to begin to take on some adult values but may still be expected to behave as a child. Young adolescents may vary greatly in the way they behave, and some of that variation will be linked to their physical development. They will be relying on themselves for control rather than on an adult, but in many ways are not ready for this. They are typically fairly argumentative as they begin to form their own ideas and identities.

Eleven-year-olds may appear quite emotionally unstable, becoming suddenly angry or laughing hysterically. They may express anger through damaging property (especially bedroom doors) or even hitting others. In fact, young people in this age group are typically not very good at taking care of themselves or their possessions. Their rooms may be untidy, with even their favourite clothes strewn about the floor. They are tired, but hate going to bed and dislike getting up. However, they are usually better at school than at home, sometimes enjoying competing with others. By now young adolescents are becoming more logical in their thinking and this will extend to matters outside their direct experience.

By 12 years of age there may be a certain amount of settling down so that the adolescent appears more eager to please. School can be very important to this age group as they begin to work more independently and become involved in discussions. Some of the extremes apparent at age 11 years are now evident in other ways, so that the 12-year-old may seem very enthusiastic about ideas or hate them. There is an increased interest in the opposite sex although 'going out' with someone commonly involves no actual outings! When 12-year-olds become angry they may still use physical ways to demonstrate their anger, despite being capable of asserting themselves verbally.

As adolescents reach 13 years they may become more introspective. This is a moody, sulky age as teenagers adjust to a new view of themselves, which may involve a lot of time in front of a mirror. This age group may be very keen not to be identified with their parents, and are usually very argumentative even about straightforward facts. Their anger may turn to tears (which they will find embarrassing), therefore they are likely to sulk and storm out of the room before they reach this point. However, they are increasing in concentration, self-control and the ability to organize themselves. It is important in therapy that the young teenager feels a sense of control over what is going on, and working together will improve chances of the programme being considered valid and worthy of effort. Therefore, it is vital to work hard to fully engage a person of this age.

14–16 years

As children proceed through adolescence they are likely to have fewer specific fears but more worries that may be associated with school and the future. This is especially true of this age group with the pressure of school examinations. Fourteen-year-olds appear more outgoing and generally enjoy life better. They seem friendly and responsible, especially to those outside the family. Even with their parents, relationships are less conflicting when parents are able to give them age-appropriate responsibility. Where there is conflict with parents or others, 14-year-olds are likely to resort to sarcasm, swearing or name calling, often under their breath. There may be a surge of aggressive impulses but it is also a time of increasing self-control. It helps greatly that the 14-year-old is becoming more objective and able to see another's point of view.

The peer group is very important and teenagers may want to spend many hours on the telephone, which gives them more time with friends. It also offers the chance to flirt with a member of the opposite sex with no risk of immediate consequences.

Fifteen-year-olds seem to lose some of their enthusiasm and become rather apathetic and indifferent. In fact they are going through another stage of introspection. There are life choices and decisions to be made and so naturally adolescents are concentrating on sorting out their own thoughts, feelings and opinions. There may be an increased tolerance of others at this age as teenagers become more sure of their own beliefs and values.

By the time adolescents reach the age of 16 years they have generally become more self-reliant, with a sense of direction. They should be less sensitive to criticism or advice and more capable in many spheres of life. By now they will have become more socially skilled and will know how to resolve conflicts successfully. If they have been given the right opportunities they should have sufficient life skills to look after themselves independently. For adolescents of this age, therapy is best presented as a series of choices to be made, so that they have the responsibility of direction. For example, provide them with information and possible options, and let them look at the costs and benefits of each.

Many adolescents enjoy looking towards their future and examining their own thoughts, which makes activities involving the past and the future very suitable for this age group.

Further Reading

ARCHER, C. (1997) *First Steps in Parenting the Child who Hurts* and ARCHER, C. (1999) Next Steps in Parenting the Child who Hurts. London: Jessica Kingsley Publishers.

Published for Adoption UK, these books are written mainly for adoptive parents, by an adoptive parent. They are easy to read and are full of practical advice on understanding and bringing up children who are placed in new families on a long-term basis. The first title is for early childhood and the second continues the age range up into adolescence.

ELLIOT, M. (1994) *Keeping Safe*, 4th edn. London: Hodder and Stoughton.

Written for parents to help them teach their children how to keep safe, this book includes advice on protecting children from abuse and also covers important areas such as drugs and bullying.

FAHLBERG, V.I. (1994) *A Child's Journey through Placement* (UK edn). London: British Agencies for Adoption and Fostering.

This book is a key text for anyone working with children who have moved families. It contains information about the behavioural and emotional problems that can arise in children who are in care and how to help children to overcome them. It includes helpful advice on working with children and carers, including life story work.

HOWE, D., BRANDON, M., HININGS, D. AND SCHOFIELD, G. (1999) *Attachment Theory, Child Maltreatment and Family Support. A Practice and Assessment Model*. London: Macmillan Press Ltd.

Howe and his colleagues have written a specialized book in which the first section covers attachment theory in detail and the second section links theory to practice. It provides a step-by-step guide to an assessment, formulation and intervention model for use when working with children who have been abused and their carers.

RYAN, A. AND WALKER, R. (1993) *Life Story Work*. London: British Agencies for Adoption and Fostering.

Here we have a very useful comprehensive guide for both professionals and adoptive or foster parents embarking on life story work with children. It emphasizes the need for whoever undertakes the work to have space, time and access to expertise. It also covers life story work with children who may have special needs.

WHEAL, A.(Ed.) (1999) *The RHP Companion to Foster Care*. Lyme Regis: Russell House Publishing.

This is a collection of chapters from a wide variety of authors who are working with children in care either directly or through research. The subjects range from looking at the child in care, through to foster care practice and discussion of issues. It is a very useful book for professionals wanting a wide number of angles on the subject.

References

American Psychiatric Association (1994) *Diagnostic and Statistical Manual of Mental Disorders* (4th edn). Washington, DC: American Psychiatric Association.

Bowlby, J (1995) *A Secure Base; Clinical Applications of Attachment Theory*. London: Routledge.

Brinich, P. (1990) Adoption, ambivalence and mourning: clinical and theoretical inter-relationships. *Adoption & Fostering*, 14 (1), 6–16.

Department of Health (1991) *Patterns and Outcomes in Child Placement*. London: HMSO.

Fahlberg, V. (1994) *A Child's Journey through Placement*. London: BAAF.

Hajal, F. and Rosenberg, E.B. (1991) The family life cycle in adoptive families. *American Journal of Orthopsychiatry*, 61 (1), 78–85.

Hobday, A. (2001) Timeholes: a useful metaphor when explaining unusual or bizarre behaviour in children who have moved families. *Clinical Child Psychology and Psychiatry*, 6 (1), 41–47.

Hobday, A. and Ollier, K. (1998) *Creative Therapy: Activities with Children and Adolescents*. Oxford: BPS Blackwell.

Howe, D., Brandon, M., Hinings, D. and Schofield, G. (1999) *Attachment Theory, Child Maltreatment and Family Support. A Practice and Assessment Model*. London: Macmillan Press Ltd.

Klaus, M.H. and Kennell, J.H. (1976) *Maternal–Infant Bonding*. St. Louis, MO: C.V. Mosby.

Main, M., Kaplan, N. and Cassidy, J. (1985) Security in infancy, childhood and adulthood: a move to the level of representation. In I. Bretherton and E. Waters (Eds) *Monographs of the Society for Research in Child Development*, Serial 209, 66–204. Chicago, IL: University of Chicago Press.

Ollier, K. and Hobday, A. (1999) *Creative Therapy 2: Working with Parents*. Oxford: BPS Blackwell.

Ryan, T. and Walker, R. (1993) *Life Story Work*. London: British Agencies for Adoption & Fostering.

Stevenson, J. (1999) The treatment of the long-term sequelae of child abuse. *Child Psychology and Psychiatry*, 40 (1), 89–111.

Index to Activities

Subject Index